DAOI
THE W
NAT

A SELECTION FROM THE ANCIEN
BEARING THE NAMES OF

Lao Zi, Lie Zi, Zhuang Zi,
Guan Yin Zi and Huai Nan Zi.

ISBN 1897853 54 8

DAOISM: THE WAY OF NATURE.

A SELECTION FROM THE ANCIENT TEXTS BEARING THE NAMES OF

Lao Zi, Lie Zi, Zhuang Zi, Guan Yin Zi and Huai Nan Zi.

COMPILED AND TRANSLATED FROM THE WORKS OF

Léon Wieger

WITH AN INTRODUCTION BY

Derek Bryce

Published by the author,
reprinted in 2006,
& distributed by

Llanerch press, Cribyn.

CONTENTS

PREFACE

The aim of this book is to present the reader with a selection of texts of the pure Daoism of the ancient writings, arranged in a meaningful order. The selections have been made primarily from the books bearing the names of three famous Daoists; Lao Zi, Lie Zi, and Zhuang Zi, but there are also a few texts from the writings of other ancient Daoists including Guan Yin Zi and Huai Nan Zi. One of the advantages of making such a selection is that texts from several authors on the same subject can be presented together. Another reason for presenting a selection is that the ancient books were written on bamboo strips tied together, and the ties often broke up with the passage of time. The texts were not always reassembled in the original order, and sometimes Confucian passages, or Daoist writings of an inferior order, were interpolated. This is especially true of the longer books of Lie Zi and Zhuang Zi in which one can find passages diametrically opposed to what was the certain teaching of the authors. The selection given here has been made with the intention of avoiding some of the problems which come with the complete works of these authors. I have however, retained some of the long anecdotes from the later chapters of the book of Zhuang Zi which are probably not the work of the Master himself, but later additions; they are by lesser Daoist writers, and show how the brief anecdotes of the original work could be developed into full length stories.

The texts are translated from the works of Léon Wieger, notably from his *Histoire des Croyances Religieuses et des Opinions Philosophiques en Chine* (Xian Xian 1913) and *Les Pères du système Taoiste* (Xian Xian, 1917). Of the many translators of Daoist works into European languages during the first half of the 20th century, the great orientalist Ananda Coomaraswamy said there were only a handful that had really understood the Chinese way of thinking; he listed a few Germans and two Frenchmen, Matgioi (Albert de Pourvoirville) and Léon Wieger, but he did not include any of the English or American translators. Dr. Wieger's translations have also the benefit of the fact that he lived most of his adult life in China at a time when it was still possible to consult living traditional scholars. He also used the traditional Chinese commentaries which are indispensable for understanding these old texts. In his translations Dr. Wieger looked into the ancient meanings of key words, and translated them accordingly. Thus Dao is translated as the Principle from its ancient meaning, and not the Way which is its meaning in modern Chinese. This is something which has been overlooked by most of the modern translators, even though the Principle makes more sense in many of the translated contexts of Dao. Lionel Giles, in *Musings of a Chinese Mystic*, thought that right at the beginning Dao came from Tian Dao, the Way of Heaven (as opposed to the way of man), and that the Tian was dropped leaving Dao standing for the First Cause, the great unseen Principle, and that this transition of meaning is to be seen in the work of Lao Zi. Giles also added that in the book of Zhuang Zi, Dao never seems to mean the Way, although it sometimes implies the Virtue of the Principle rather than the Principle itself. The Chinese word 'de' is generally translated as virtue, but Wieger stated that its ancient meaning was action (but the action of Dao is also, in a sense, its virtue). Thus the famous book of Lao Zi could be called *A Treatise on the Principle and its Action* rather than *A Treatise on the Way and Virtue*. Léon Wieger also used the word sage to describe the Daoists, a meaningful term which has not always been used by other translators, (but he also used the same word to designate scholars who had mere book learning so that the reader must interpret 'sage' according to the context). Most of this, I think, justifies rendering Léon Wieger's translation into English. When Wieger was translating the ancient books he seems to have become, as it were, Chinese, with enthusiasm for his subject; his only drawback in his books is that when he stepped back to make personal comments, he reverted to his background, that of a European scholar of his times, and a Christian. I have left his personal observations out of this work; they are not needed for his translations, but I have retained his summaries of the old Chinese commentaries which accompanied some of the chapters of Lao Zi. Readers should note that where Wieger uses the term 'evolution' this is not meant in a Darwinian sense, or in the Spencerian one of indefinite human progress; in this book evolution means either the unfolding of events in time, or the progress of the being across successive lives and incarnations, leading towards perfection. There are no genders in written Chinese but like most other translators of his period, Wieger tended to use masculine terms; in rendering his work into English I have tried to rectify some of this, for example by using the plural 'sages' with 'they' rather than Wieger's singular 'sage' with 'he.' I hope readers will bear in mind that use of the word man in these translations implies humanity as a whole. I would also add that the yin-yang symbol shows perfect symmetry between the male and female principles, and that where the texts speak of heaven being superior to earth, male to female, they elsewhere speak of heaven collaborating with earth to produce beings, and they say that yin, earth, the female principle, is the inherent state of Dao, whereas yang, heaven, the male principle, is the state of Dao in time, and is in some ways inappropriate. In other words heaven is superior to earth in the visible spatial symbolism, but earth is anterior to heaven in temporal symbolism (for the corporeal state is said to symbolize the non-manifest). Thus the relationship of male and female depends on the point of view; heaven, the male principle is above earth, but earth, the female principle is, in a sense, before heaven!

The purpose of this book is to provide a meaningful introduction to Daoism by means of a selection of ancient texts. Thus there is only a short introduction, followed by collected anecdotes from the books of Lie Zi and Zhuang Zi, chapters on the way of the sage, Dao, the Principle (the Way), and de, the action or virtue of the Principle. The *Dao De Jing* of Lao Zi is the oldest definitive book of Daoism, but it is concise to the point of obscurity, and later authors such as Lie Zi and Zhuang ZI rectified this problem by explaining difficult points or abstruse questions by means of anecdotes. It is for this reason that I have put the anecdotes near the beginning of the book, and not, as logic might suggest, at the end. I hope this method of letting the old texts speak for themselves will appeal to all seekers after truth, and that this little book will be of some use to them. Chinese names are in Pinyin except for older references. The word Daoism throughout is used to describe the pure Daoism of the ancient sages, and not its later politico-religious developments. Many of these translations were first published in *Wisdom of the Daoist Masters,* 1984.

Derek Bryce, 1994.

1. INTRODUCTION

Prologue:

It is difficult to define Daoism by any simple formula, and in fact it is easier to say what it is not than what it is. It is not a 'system' of any kind and certainly not a religion in the sense in which the western religions of Semitic origin are understood; it should not, however be described as atheistic, but as non-theistic. The old Daoists tended to ignore or bypass the notion of God, the Sovereign on High whom the ancient Chinese people imagined as a material being sitting on a throne in a cloud-palace, administering after the manner of the Chinese empire. The Daoists sometimes refer to Heaven which denotes the Essence, and rarely to the Sovereign. Dao is the absolute, beyond being, that beyond which one cannot conceive, the great unseen Principle. The old sages do not claim any origin of Daoism by divine revelation, but that it is a rational way derived from the observation of natural phenomena.

Daoism 'surfaced' into history in China around 500 B.C. with the appearance of its first known written text attributed to Lao Zi, the Old Master. I say 'surfaced' because there were Daoists before that time that have left us little more than their names. To try to begin to understand Daoism it is necessary to 'taste' it initially by reading a representative sample of the old texts, which is what I have tried to provide in this book. I continue this introduction with a brief historical survey so that the reader can understand the conditions in which Daoism appeared and also know the names of a few characters from Chinese history that are mentioned in some of the texts quoted later in this book.

Setting the scene; ancient times:

The chronological period of Chinese history begins around the twenty-fifth century B.C., but there are legends which refer to pre-historic times. In common with some other ancient and traditional peoples, the Chinese have a legend of primordial times when there was a single humanity with one language and tradition. The Chinese situate this primordial humanity in the region of the Pamir, a dissected plateau to the north of Tibet (but this could refer to a later stage of pre-history, and not necessarily be the original location). They say that the people eventually migrated out in different directions, to the west, the south, the east, and that with geographical isolation and the passage of time, language, customs and traditions came to differ. For their own pre-history, the Chinese speak of three legendary names; Fu Xi the shepherd, Shen Nong the farmer, and Huang Di, often called the Yellow Emperor (but more correctly the Yellow Sovereign for he pre-dates the Chinese empire). He can also be called Lord of the Earth, for yellow is the colour of the Chinese loess. Fu Xi represents the age of wandering nomads, living by stock rearing, hunting and fishing. The age of Shen Nong represents a semi-nomadic stage of allied clans depending on agricultural plots for much of their subsistence. Huang Di, the Yellow Emperor, represents the definitive sedentary state when the allied clans of the Xia settled permanently under a single great chief or sovereign, and when the heads of the clans had become feudal lords.

There are two systems of chronology for the ancient dates of Chinese History, down to 827 B.C. They are the known as the conventional chronology which relied for ancient times on the calculations of Liu Xin, and the traditional chronology. The latter is based on a manuscript known as the Chronicle Written on Bamboo, which was buried in a tomb in 299 B.C., and dug up in 281 A.D., thereby escaping the destruction of ancient archives which took place in 213 B.C. Dates from the traditional chronology will be given in this book. Wieger expressed the opinion that the traditional chronology inspired more confidence because the dates in it were admitted before the destruction of the ancient archives when verification by cross-referencing with other archives was still possible. The discrepancies between the two chronologies are not very great, 216 years for the accession of Yu the Great, marking the beginning of the first dynasty; and from 827 B.C. onwards they coincide. The Yellow Sovereign (alias Emperor) cannot be dated accurately, but he seems to have reigned sometime between the thirtieth and twenty fifth centuries B.C. Before that time we have only legend. The accession of Emperor Yao, in 2145 B.C., appears to be a fairly certain date. Yao abdicated in 2073 B.C., in favour of Shun, and died in 2045. Shun died in 1992, leaving the empire to Yu the Great, whose reign began in

1989 B.C., after a period of official mourning. In this early period new emperors were nominated by the previous one, with the approval of the feudal lords, or were chosen by the latter. Yu the Great put an end to this state of affairs by appointing his own son as successor, thereby making the position hereditary and commencing the first dynasty (of the Xia) which lasted from 1989 to 1554 B.C. One of the Daoist authors described this as Yu stealing the empire and giving it to his family! We shall see in the texts later that the Daoists looked back with nostalgia to the pre-dynastic times when there was peace and almost imperceptible government. The Daoists praised the Yellow Emperor for many things, but criticised him for others, especially for having made the first war. They saw Yao and Shun as praise-worthy at times, but as the instigators of the perversion of human nature by making laws and replacing the natural with the artificial or conventional, a process which they say has gone on and on since those times.

What has survived in the Annals of this early period enables us to form a picture of the organization of the empire, and of its ancient theism. At the top was the emperor with his ministers and officials, then the feudal lords, and finally the people. The emperor held the mandate of heaven so long as he governed well. Thus a good emperor feared and respected the people lest he should lose the favour of heaven. The ancient theism envisaged at the top a supreme being, the Sovereign on High, Heaven. These two names denote one and the same being, for the term Sovereign on High represents the power of God, the term Heaven symbolizes the essence. Below the Sovereign, were the glorified Manes which included the *shen*, celestial Genii which float about freely in space, and the *zhi*, terrestrial Genii that are fixed each in one place; finally there were the inglorious Manes completing the invisible hierarchy.

The rôle of the emperor was twofold, temporal and spiritual. He acted as high priest for his people and he was their mediator with Heaven. For the good of the people he honoured and sacrificed to Heaven, the Sovereign on High. Likewise he invoked the Genii of the mountains and rivers, and bowed to the Genii of the localities. The empire was divided up into four regions, in each of which there was a high mountain functioning as a secondary temporal and spiritual centre. Once every five years, the emperor came out from his centre, his capital, to visit each of the four regions. Anyone who has seen a photograph of the near-vertical cliffs to be climbed to reach the top of one of these mountains, Mount Hwa, will realise that the emperors had to be physically tough and active to accomplish this, and some of them reached a ripe old age. Back in the nineteen thirties, Peter Goullert attempted to climb Mount Hwa, assisted by the chains that had been hung in place there in modern times, but he ended up being hauled up like a sack of potatoes by his Chinese guides.

On the top of each mountain the emperor lit a pyre to inform Heaven of his presence, and he bowed to the mountains and rivers of the region, to the Genii. He would also use such ceremonies for temporal purposes, conferring with the lords gathered there, confirming or renewing investitures, and so on. The importance attached to these ceremonies by the ancient Chinese is indicated by a text from 1050 B.C. concerning the ending of the second dynasty by the overthrowing of the tyrant Xin. Fa of Chou who commanded the coalition that overthrew Xin, accused the latter as having neglected to make the offerings to Heaven on behalf of the nation and thereby having forfeited his mandate. After his victory Fa set up the third dynasty of the Chou which lasted till 256 B.C.

(As a point of interest there is a striking resemblance between this division of ancient China into a supreme centre in which the emperor resided, and four secondary regions, and the ancient division of Ireland into a centre Tara, where the high king resided, and four kingdoms [of the four masters] around it. This is especially significant as there is an ancient Chinese legend about a voyage across the western ocean to a far-off green island, described as a land of four masters.)

The emperor used large turtle-shells for the practice of official divination, to inquire if things were being done according to the will of heaven.

The lords themselves also took a subordinate part in this official worship of heaven and the Genii, each in their own jurisdiction and within prescribed limits. The people were only permitted to take part in this official worship as spectators. Their own public worship was of the local Patron of the Earth, at the mound of each village. This local Patron or Genie was said to be delegated by the Genie of the region, who was delegated by the one of the empire, who was delegated by Heaven, a hierarchy of the invisible world parallel with that of the visible one.

Apart from the public worship outlined above, there was the private worship of the ancestors, by all the families from the emperor downwards. Offerings were made to the ancestors, and pictographs on ancient bronzes tell us that the Chinese believed that they came down to savour these offerings, although, of course, they did not eat them. The ancestors were informed of events and intentions, and their blessings sought. Emperor Shun appointed an official musician with a view to establishing relations between Genii, Manes, and humans, so that the object of music for the ancients was as a sacred art. They used music to call the ancestors to the family temples prior to making offerings there.

Such was the ancient worship, and it was considered important to keep it in its original purity. Thus Shun, before the year 2073 B.C., whilst Yao was still emperor, took military action against two tribes, the Li and the Miao. The ancient Chinese had come into close contact with these tribes, who had other customs, a different religion, and were addicted to fetishism and magic. Shun appointed two persons to sever the communications between heaven and earth, so that there was no more descending and visiting. "The two categories of Genii and human beings should each have its own habitat. Each ought to remain in its own home. When humans offer the official worship to the Genii, the Genii bless them and the humans are happy. That is the only relationship that is permitted. The Li and the Miao disturbed this peace. Genii and humans intermingled. Everyone took to making offerings to the Genii, and asked favours of them through special evokers. From this there resulted an indecent promiscuity." Shun caused these unofficial relations between heaven and earth to be broken off, and re-established the ancient national worship, which lasted until the time when the third dynasty fell into decay (770 B.C.). After that the ancient worship was finally perverted. (There is a parallel to be seen with the above in the early Christian period of the Celtic parts of the West, where some of the saints complained of people having relationships with non-humans; these beliefs persisted into the middle ages, where Merlin and Morgan-le-Fay are depicted as half-human in the largely fictional Arthurian romances.)

Confucius and Lao Zi:

Following the decay of the ancient theism, two names stand out in the history of the Chinese people, Confucius and Lao Zi. Confucius was born in 551, and died in 479 B.C. The precise dates of Lao Zi, the Old Master, are not known; he was older than Confucius, and he must have lived between 570 and 490 B.C.

Confucius established for the Chinese people what may be termed a social way, based primarily on filial piety, the family, with the idea of the emperor as head of a super-family, and with emphasis on etiquette, rites and music. He rescued some ancient books from oblivion, the Annals, Odes, Rites and Music, and the Book of Changes or Mutations. From them he made a system of human behaviour. The Daoists criticize him for having turned the ancient ways into a fixed and conventional system, with no adaptation to changed circumstances, and for having replaced the natural virtues with artificial goodness and fairness. Confucianism, however, seems to have suited the majority of the Chinese people up to fairly recent times. In the old Daoist writings, especially the books of Lie Zi and Zhuang Zi, Confucius is presented in two main poses; first as the destroyer of naturalism and creator of artificiality, second as being converted to Daoism and teaching a doctrine quite different from his own. These are genuine Daoist texts but they must not be imputed to the historical Confucius; they are literary devices used by the Daoists to ridicule Confucius, or to show him as advocating Daoism before the end of his life, something for which there is no historical proof, although there are some texts describing meetings between Lao Zi and Confucius which may have a historical basis. There are also a few non-authentic texts which extol Confucius or Confucianism without reservation, and they are interpolations. Despite the apparent conflict, it is a fact of Chinese history that Confucianism and Daoism, in its later developments, have existed side by side over long periods of time.

Lao Zi was the author of the first treatise on Daoism. The Daoist tradition tells us that he was an archivist at the court of the Zhou emperor, but that he became weary of the decadent state of the Chinese empire, and decided to leave it. When he was about to cross the Western Pass, he was delayed by his friend Yin Xi, guardian of the pass, and persuaded to write his famous treatise, *Dao de Jing*, the fundamental book of Daoism. Some have doubted if Lao

Zi ever existed, or wrote. The Daoist tradition strongly affirms that he did, and the great historian Sima Qian said of him that, having loved obscurity above all, this man deliberately effaced the traces of his life. Lao Zi did not invent Daoism, he is said to have found it in the archives of the third ministry, which included material coming from outside China; however there seem to have been Daoists in China before Lao Zi, but no writings have come down from them. This implies that something quite similar to Daoism had existed during the time of the ancient theism, as the esoteric or secret part of the Chinese tradition. The ancient Daoism as we know it, with its emphasis on a spiritual way whilst living a normal life without complex rites, and without forming a separate sect, is perhaps as close as one can come in historical times to the primordial tradition of this humanity. Of the other ancient Daoists, we have already mentioned Guan Yin Zi (Yin Xi). Two other famous ancient Daoists were Lie Zi who was born around 438 B.C., and Zhuang Zi who was in the decline of his life by 330 B.C. Each of these sages developed the concise teaching of Lao Zi by resort to anecdotes which made obscure points easier to understand. Lie Zi did not write, but the book bearing his name is probably based on notes taken down by his followers. I have also included quotes from the book known as the *Huai Nan Zi* which was collected or purchased by a prince of Zheng who died in 122 B.C.

Daoism:

Dao cannot in truth be named; it is the Absolute, Formlessness, the Principle, that beyond which one cannot conceive. In the texts it is sometimes called a being, but in reality it is beyond being. The texts say that words cannot describe it, and readers must make the necessary mental transposition when they see the term 'being' which is used to avoid literary clumsiness. The old Daoists said that everything happens 'as though there is a lord governor of the universe provided that this does not imply a distinct material being.' They said 'it is the norm inherent in the universe,' and sometimes they used the term Heaven for this, which to the Chinese implies the unique essence. (They generally avoided using the theistic term Sovereign on High, because, as implied above, the latter was taken too literally and materially in the minds of the Chinese.)

After Dao come the yin and the yang represented by a beautiful symmetrical symbol. Yin represents concentration, earth, passivity, female; yang represents expansion, heaven, activity and male. Yin is the inherent state of Dao, yang is its state in time. The yin-yang or heaven-earth binomial produces all sentient beings through *de*, the action or virtue of Dao, the Principle.

The Daoists see life and death as two phases of the same being, and they consider the majority as trapped in an endless chain of successive lives and deaths, with a longer or shorter period spent in "the great dormitory between heaven and earth" before each rebirth. Rebirth involves loss of memory of the previous existence, and of the previous individuality. Conscious survival after death is only for those who have perfected themselves during successive lives, have exhausted their bad karma, and have come to acquire a permanent spiritual state. Like other eastern peoples, the Daoists see karma as an inexorable natural law, rather than as an angry personal God doling out punishments.

If Confucianism can be described as a social way, then Daoism can be said to be a rational way, although it is, above all, spiritual or intellectual (in the true sense of that word) and esoteric or hidden. The Daoist sages claim a rational origin for their way, which they say is based on the observation of natural phenomena. Thus heaven and earth produce all beings without doing anything, without wearing themselves out, so the sages place emphasis on non-action, only acting when they are constrained to do so. This non-action has been seen by some superficial translators as implying laziness and inertia; in reality it implies restraint from external action in order to concentrate on the inward life of self improvement. In all traditions there are those who take everything literally, and no doubt there have been some self-styled Daoists who have taken non-action literally and used it as an excuse for a life of laziness, but this is far from the truth in the case of the genuine masters of the way. The same applies to the Daoist notion of apathy, which is based on superior knowledge, on not wishing to act in such a way as to add to the existing confusion, or in a futile way; this is quite different from the apathy of an inferior order, from the couldn't-care-less attitude of indolent and insensitive types. The same applies to Daoist indifference, to which we may add that even in the Christian West there have been recognized saints who were characterized by an attitude of 'holy indifference'... Coming back to natural phenomena, the Daoists observe the constant illumination of the sun and the moon; that they shine on all and everyone. The conclusion is that the sage should treat everyone with the same benevolence, and shine with a tempered light to avoid eclipsing the sun and the moon, to avoid making a show.

The Daoists laughed at rites, moral and social rules of behaviour and the like, but this does not imply that they were not moral or virtuous. On the contrary they laughed at conventional morality because they had, from their inner ascendancy, a natural morality that is superior to the exterior rules laid down by a religion or society. Those moderns who think they can become amoral and do what they please by styling themselves Daoists are off the mark. One of the modern Daoists, Hua-ching Ni, has pointed out that conventional morality is derived from the natural truth, and it should be respected until one reaches the natural morality that comes with a state of high spiritual and intellectual awareness. Natural morality, for example, would consider speculation to be immoral, whereas educated or conventional morality often condones speculation and acquisitiveness at the expense of others. Likewise natural morality would say it is wrong to kill others simply because their religion, culture, tribe, or ethnic group is different. The history of colonial expansion in Africa, Asia and the New World shows us how artificial morality, even conventional religious morality, has condoned atrocious acts against non-Europeans. Quite recent internal troubles in countries of Europe and Africa serve to demonstrate that nothing in modern times has changed peoples' hostile attitudes to ethnic or tribal groups other than their own. The Daoist sages say that the ancient emperors falsified morality when they said that although one should not kill, it was all right to do so in warfare, because then one was not killing people but brigands!

In politics, the Daoists followed the plan of interfering as little as possible. Lao Zi said that governing the empire was like cooking very small fish; one should proceed with great delicacy, otherwise they would break up. The Daoist attitude to human affairs was to stick to simplicity and not to encourage innovations, but once innovations had come in they would use them for they recognized that one had to adapt to the times, to bend with the wind, and that one cannot set the clock back. As Lao Zi said to Confucius, you cannot change the (black) crows of today into the (white) geese of yesterday. Despite their retirement, when times were favourable the ancient sages even consented to be ministers in the government, but when times were politically bad, their aim was to become hidden amongst the mass of the people, or lost in the countryside as subsistence farmers, concentrating on their own interior development, in which there is enough to occupy one for a lifetime. There were times when the Daoists had influence on politics. In the Book of Zhuang Zi we find that there are people who stand on tiptoe looking over the others' shoulders for a bargain, who push their desire for profit even so far as to lose the love of their fellow citizens, and that for this they are despised. Thus we find there was a period when businessmen were not allowed to take part in official ceremonies, and had to build their houses outside the towns and cities. The ancient Daoists rejected political parties on the grounds that they were each so preoccupied in criticizing the faults of those opposing them that they forgot, or failed to see, the faults of their own system. They said that each item of political concern should be examined on its own merits and not according to the dogma or theory of any fixed system. Likewise they also avoided all science, that is to say systems of knowledge, including traditional sciences such as alchemy. Alchemy seems to have come into Daoism later on, and Lao Zi is then often presented as its patron. We would add, in any case, that the most profound aim of alchemy, the transmutation of the base human being (lead) into a superior being (gold) is, and always has been the aim of all esoteric ways.

The great Persian poet 'Attār, in *the Conference of the Birds*, wrote as follows: The Simurgh flew over China, and one of its feathers fell on that land. They all made a picture of it, and from it they each formed their own system of ideas and so fell into confusion. This feather is still in the picture-gallery of that country; hence the saying, 'seek knowledge even in China.' The Simurgh is a mysterious giant bird that is gifted with all knowledge. A feather of the Simurgh therefore indicates sacred writing. The fact that everyone made a picture of the feather implies that the Chinese sacred writing is descended from the original or primordial version. We can thus interpret the saying as implying that the primordial tradition, or something close to it, can be found in ancient Chinese writings. This can surely be interpreted as referring to the Daoist writings. It does not, however, imply that those who understand this should go off and become Daoists, but rather that people can learn something of value from it whatever their religion, tradition or beliefs, especially in modern times, and this is certainly the view of the present writer. Furthermore, the books that have come down to us only represent the exterior or exoteric teachings of Daoism, and do not include the esoteric practices.

What hints at the primordial nature of Daoism is that it is an esoteric way not encumbered by rites, rules and regulations, but in which the Daoist must be virtuous and therefore practise natural morality. Apart from the practice of natural virtue, the spiritual method or practice of the ancient Daoists was to sit cross-legged and totally empty the mind, so that they each became empty like a cup or vessel, open above to receive the 'influx of heaven'. They described the first effect of this as feeling as though an unguent had been spread in a sort of halo around the head. In modern times such a technique of emptying one's mind is difficult to practise, and the recommendations from other sources such as Indian cosmology and the *Ramayana* are that the only methods suitable for our present time will be invocatory ones, the repetition of a sacred phrase or name, such as a mantra (Sanskrit), *dhikr* (Arabic), or the prayer of the heart (Orthodox Christianity). There are mantras that are used by modern Daoists. The reason for invocatory methods is that it is easier for the mind of modern man to become still through concentrating on the repetition of a sacred phrase, than by simply trying to empty itself. It is a method that 'works' providing it is practised with suspension of thought, without the mind wandering, which is never easy, but the invocation itself helps one to attain this. The effectiveness of this method, which at first glance seems pointless, is that the element of repetition puts the being in communion with the great rhythms of the cosmos, such as the waves of the oceans, the flow of the tides, the progress of the seasons in the macrocosm, and the breathing cycle and regular beating of the heart in the microcosm, effecting a harmony with them. Experience shows that it 'works,' but it is one of those things where the proof of the pudding is in the eating, and no amount of verbiage will ever resolve any argument about it. The ancient Daoists were generally married and lived amongst the people; they did not form a band apart nor did they have monasteries with rules, but young aspiring Daoists would often spend some years in the house of a master, a term which should always imply a teacher (and not someone who is seeking power over others as in some modern self-styled 'masters'). Later on, Daoist monastic sects appeared, despite the fact that the early Daoists had stressed that they should not form a sect apart, but live amongst the people or in the country. Some of the monastic groups deviated considerably from the ancient Daoism, but others, such as the Lungmen sect remained close to the teaching of Lao Zi. The ancient texts imply that the peoples' abuse of sex was the biggest factor contributing to the shortening of human life. Bao

Pu Zi a later Daoist, added that though the sages were married, they did not indulge in sexual activity too often. The same writer also added that the ancient writers did not comment on this private matter out of a sense of decency. The ancient Daoists also seem to have practised breathing exercises, but they did not go to the extremes of the crazy imitators of Peng Zu who aided their breathing "by gestures similar to those of a climbing bear or a bird in flight" (Zhuang Zi).

The Daoists were also careful to watch over their interior, refusing access into their minds to any thoughts and suggestions that would disturb their inner peace. Such thoughts, coming from without through their sense organs or within from their memory or imagination, they would reject before they would become a problem. They said that the sages never had any problems because they always dealt with them in their earliest and weakest beginnings. Zhuang Zi said that it is within the power of anyone to practise this method provided that one's mind 'neither examines nor discusses what is presented to it, but simply refuses it access.' Thus the sages maintained their interior peace. This does not, of course, mean that they never had thoughts; it simply means that when they did wish to use their minds, they were refreshed, uncluttered and ready for the task. Zhuang Zi illustrates this by pointing out that those who have very expensive and special swords keep them wrapped in silks in a box, and only bring them out for use on special occasions. He goes on to say that people's minds are more precious than any sword, yet by giving their imaginations free rein and using their minds all the time on frivolities they become blunted and worn.

Zhuang Zi said that peace can be found in the hustle and bustle of this world, provided one knows how to keep in harmony with the cosmic movement, just as a duck calmly bobs up and down with the swell on the water. Although, the Daoists sought internal peace, they were realists and not sentimentalists with regard to the world at large, regarding which Zhuang Zi said that perfect peace can only be achieved from the day when the people seek the cause of their own ills in their own interior imperfection.

What can be said of the ancient Daoism, at the risk of repetition, is that it comes as close as one can find to what might have been the primordial tradition of this humanity, a tradition which is hidden in the centre of all traditions, but which is here plain to be seen. It has sometimes been referred to as the Perennial Philosophy. Its importance to our times cannot be stressed too much, but sadly, few will understand this.

2. ANECDOTES

The frog of the well:

(The following story illustrates the difference between the exoteric point of view, that of the frog [a Confucian], and the esoteric, represented by the turtle [a Daoist]).

Do you know the story of the frog of the old well and the turtle of the eastern sea? "How happy I am in my well," said the frog to the turtle; "I can jump on the edge, hide in the holes between the bricks, swim on the surface or dive into the mud. None of the inhabitants of this well, larvae and tadpoles, can do that much; therefore I prefer my well to your sea; why don't you come and try some of its charms." To please the frog, the turtle tried. But the well was so narrow that once its right foot was in, it was impossible for it to get its left foot in. After having withdrawn its foot, it gave the frog the following information about the sea: "Its length is more than a thousand *li* and it is deeper than the height of a thousand men mounted on top of each other. At the time of emperor Yu there were nine floods in ten years; all of this water ran into the sea without augmenting it. At the time of Emperor Tang there were seven droughts in eight years; no water ran into the sea and yet it showed not the slightest diminution. Duration, quantity; these terms do not apply to the sea. This constant immobility is the charm of my home." With these words the frog of the well got vertigo and went out of his little mind. (Zhuang Zi, ch. 17)

The autumn flood:

(In this story the Genie of the River is exoteric, a Confucian, and the Genie of the Sea is esoteric and teaches him Daoism):

It was the time of the autumn flood. A hundred swollen rivers poured their waters into the Yellow River whose bed was so wide than one could not distinguish a cow from a horse on the opposite bank. The sight of this pleased the Genie of the River, who said to himself that there was nothing better in the world than his domain. Following the current, he descended as far as the North Sea. On seeing its waters, which extended eastwards without limits, he realized that there existed better domains than his, and he sighed to the Genie of the Sea: "The saying he who knows little, thinks himself great applies to me. I have certainly heard it said that there is better than Confucius and his heroes, but I did not believe it. Now that I have seen the extent of your empire, I begin to believe that your doctrine also is superior to that of Confucius. I think I have done well in coming for your teaching, otherwise the truly wise would have ended up laughing at me." "Welcome!" said the Genie of the Sea. "Yes the frog that lives in the bottom of a well has no idea of the ocean; it only knows its own hole. The mayfly hatched and dead in summer does not know what ice is; it has known only one season. A limited scholar like Confucius knows nothing of the superior science of Dao, the Principle, besotted as he is with the prejudices of his caste. Having come out from your narrow bed you have seen the ocean without limits; convinced now of your imperfection you have become capable of learning the superior teaching. Listen! Of all the waters the greatest is the ocean. Innumerable rivers pour into it without cease, yet they never augment it. It flows out continuously through the eastern straits, without diminishing. It neither floods nor shrinks as do the great rivers; its level is always the same, invariable. Such is my empire. Ah well, its immensity has never inspired any pride in me. Why, because in comparison with heaven and earth, with the physical cosmos, I find it small. I feel myself to be no more than a stone or a shrub on a mountain. Being so small, why should I esteem myself? Compared with the universe, the depths of the four oceans are reduced to little holes in an immense surface. Compared with the earth, our China is reduced to dimensions proportional to that of a grain in an enormous granary. If the totality of existing beings can he expressed by the number ten thousand, humanity is worth only a single unit. Nowhere, in fact, over all the inhabited earth does the proportion of humans with reference to that of other beings exceed this quantity. Therefore humanity is to the mass of the universe what a hair is to the body of a horse. There you have reduced to a straw what has so occupied the ancient sovereigns, tormented the scholars and worn out the politicians. The Confucian hero Bo Yi is reputed great for the rôle he played on this little scene; and Confucius is reputed wise for his rhetorical speeches about it. These men believed themselves to be something because they knew no better, just as you believed yourself to be the first among the aquatic genies before you had seen the sea."

Recalling the discussions of the sophists of his time on the notion of great and small, the Genie of the River said to the Genie of the Sea: "Then from now on should I consider the universe as the expression of absolute greatness, and a hair as a symbol of absolute smallness; is that so?" "No!" said the Genie of the Sea, "it is not like that. The universe existing at the present time is not the expression of absolute greatness, for its quantity is not constant. It varies with the duration of time, with the course of evolution, according to the becomings and endings of things. Envisaged thus, through high science, things change their aspect, the absolute becoming relative. Thus the difference between great and small is effaced in the vision from an infinite distance. The difference between past and present is effaced similarly, before and after disappearing in the limitless chain; and in consequence the past no longer inspires sadness and the present has no more interest. The difference between prosperity and destitution is wiped out in the same way, these ephemeral phases disappearing in the eternal evolution; and in consequence, having no longer causes any pleasure and losing no longer causes any sadness. For those who see from this distance and this height, life is no longer happiness, death is no longer a misfortune; for they know that these phases succeed one another and that nothing can last. Man is ignorant of many more things than he knows. Compared with the universe he is an infinitely small thing; wishing to conclude from the little that he knows, from the little that he is, what he does not know, the universality of beings, is a process that leads him nowhere. Do not therefore in your speculations use the hair that you are as a measure of smallness, or the changing cosmos as a measure of greatness."

Satisfied to have found so good a teacher, the Genie of the River continued his questioning: "The philosophers claim that an extremely attenuated thing becomes zero, and that the same thing extremely amplified becomes infinite. Is that true?" "Yes and no," said the Genie of the Sea. "The notions of extreme attenuation and extreme amplification cannot be established by taking one and the same thing as an example. The conceivable extreme attenuation is the abstract essence. The measurable base of amplification is concrete matter. Essence and matter are two different things which coexist in every sentient being superior to zero. Zero is that which calculation can no longer divide; the infinite is that which numbers can no longer embrace. The word 'small' describes concrete matter, thought reaches the abstract essence; beyond that come metaphysical intuitions, inner voices which, being neither matter nor essence, are known only through subjective appreciation. It is by following these metaphysical intuitions that the superior man does many things quite differently from the common man, but without despising the latter because he does not have the same enlightenment. These are the things that place him beyond honour and shame, reward and punishment. They are the things which make him forget the distinctions between great and small, good and bad. From all this, one may say:

The man of Dao keeps silent; the perfect man seeks after nothing; the great man has no longer an 'I'; for he has brought all the parts together into one, an ecstatic contemplation of universal unity."

The Genie of the River having yet again insisted, in order to learn about the distinctions between noble and vile, great and small, etc., the Genie of the Sea continued: "If one considers beings in the light of Dao the Principle, these distinctions do not exist, all being one. In their own eyes all beings are noble and consider others as vile with reference to themselves; a subjective point of view. In the eyes of the common people beings are noble or vile according to a certain routine appreciation independent of reality; a conventional point of view. Considered objectively and relatively, any being is great with reference to those smaller than itself, and any are small with reference to those greater than themselves; heaven and earth are but a grain, a hair is a mountain. Considered from the point of view of utility, all beings are useful for what they can do, all are useless for what they cannot do; the east and west coexist necessarily, by opposition, each one having attributes of its own. Finally, with reference to the taste of the observer, all beings have some side through which they please some, and another side through which they displease others; Yao and Jie each had admirers and detractors. Abdication ruined neither Yao nor Shun, whereas it ruined Baron Kuai. Revolt gave benefit to Emperors Tang and Wu, whereas it caused Duke Bo to perish. According to the times and circumstances the same actions do not give the same results; what is expedient for one, or in certain circumstances, is not for another. All of this is relative and variable. A battering ram is the best thing for breaching a rampart; whereas it would be quite unsuitable for blocking up a hole; different means. Emperor Mu's coursers could cover a thousand li a day, but they would not have been as good as a cat for catching a rat; different qualities. The owl counts its feathers and catches its lice at night whereas in daylight it cannot even see a mountain; a different nature. With stronger reason, nothing is fixed amongst moral things, esteem, opinion, etc.; they all have a double aspect. In consequence, wishing for good without evil, right without wrong, order without disorder shows that one understands nothing of the laws of the universe; it is like dreaming of a heaven without an earth, a yin without a yang. The double aspect coexists in everything. Wishing to distinguish as real entities, these two inseparable correlatives, shows a weak mind; heaven and earth are one, and likewise the opposed aspects of all contraries. Of the ancient sovereigns, some obtained the throne by succession, others by usurpation. All are called good sovereigns because they acted in conformity with the taste of the people of their times. Misunderstanding the epoch, acting contrary to the taste of one's contemporaries, that is what qualifies one to be called a usurper. Meditate on these things, Genie of the River, and you will understand that there is neither greatness nor smallness, nobility nor lowliness, good nor evil in the absolute sense; but that all these things are relative, depending on the times and circumstances, on the appreciation of people, on opportunism."

"But then," said the Genie of the River, "what should I do? What should I not do? What should I admit? What should I regret? Is there a yes or a no, a moral rule of behaviour?" "From the point of view of the Principle," replied the Genie of the Sea, "there is only an absolute unity, and changing aspects. To put anything of the absolute outside the Principle would be to err about the Principle. Therefore there is no absolute morality, but only an opportunist expedience. Practically, follow the times and circumstances. Be uniformly just as a reigning prince, beneficent like the God of the Earth, indifferent as an individual; embrace all beings, for all are one. The Principle is immutable, having had no beginning, and not having an end. Beings change, being born and dying without a stable permanence. From non-being they pass to being, without rest under any form, through the course of the years and the ages; beginnings and endings, growth and decay, succeed one another. That is all that we can ascertain, as a rule, as a law, governing beings. Their life passes on the scene of the world just as a fleeing horse passes before one's eyes; not a moment without change, without vicissitudes. And you ask what to do, what not to do? Follow the course of the transformations, act according to the circumstances of the moment; that is all there is to do."

"Finally," said the Genie of the River, "will you teach me the advantages of knowledge of the Principle?" "These advantages are as follows: Those who know the Principle know the law which derives from it, apply it as it should be applied, and are in consequence respected by all beings. Those whose conduct is thus all-wise, are not burnt by fire, drowned by water, harmed by heat or cold, nor by ferocious beasts; not that they have nothing to fear from these dangers, but because their wisdom helps them avoid all misfortune. They behave with such circumspection that no ill comes to them. This wisdom, which comes from the knowledge of the Principle, is what one calls the heavenly element (natural in man) by opposition to the human (artificial) element. For action to conform to original perfection, the heavenly element (nature) must predominate." "Would you clarify the difference between the heavenly and human" insisted the Genie of the River. "It may be explained as follows" said the Genie of the Sea. "Cattle and horses are quadrupeds; that is the heavenly element (their nature). If they have a bit in their mouth or a ring through their nose, that is the human element (which is artificial, against nature). The human must not strangle the heavenly, the artificial must not extinguish the natural; the artefact must not destroy the entity of truth. To restore one's nature is to come back to the first truth of being." (Zhuang Zi, ch.17).

Politicians; Confucius and the old fisherman.

Whilst walking in the Zi Wei forest, Confucius sat down to rest near the Xiang Tan knoll. His disciples took out their books. The master strummed his lute and began to sing. The song attracted an old fisherman. His hair uncombed, his sleeves rolled up, the old man alighted from his boat, climbed up the bank, approached, placed his left hand on his knee and his chin in his right hand, and listened attentively. When the song was finished he beckoned to Zi Gong and Zi Lu, who went over to him. "Who is he," asked the old man, indicating Confucius. "He is the sage of Lu", said Zi Lu. "What is his name," asked the old man. "Kong!" said Zi Lu. "And what does this Kong do," asked the old man. Zi Gong replied: "He endeavours to revive sincerity, loyalty, goodness and fairness, rites and music for the greatest good of the Principality of Lu and the empire." "Is he a prince," asked the old man. "No!" said Zi Gong. "Is he a minister," asked the old man. "No!" replied Zi Gong again. The old man smiled and withdrew. Zi Gong heard him murmuring: "Goodness, fairness; it's very nice no doubt but he will be lucky if he doesn't lose in this game. In any case the worry and harm he causes himself will prejudice him from true perfection by wearing out his mind and body; he is a long way from the knowledge of the Principle." Zi Gong reported these words to Confucius who quickly pushed aside the lute lying on his knees, got up saying "he is a sage," and went down the bank to ask the old man to speak with him. The latter was just leaning on his gaff in order to push his boat off. On seeing Confucius he stopped and turned towards him. Confucius approached him saluting. "What do you want of me," the old man asked him. Confucius said: "You have just said something which I do not quite understand. I respectfully beg you to teach me kindly for my benefit." "This desire is most praiseworthy," said the old man. Confucius bowed down, then, having straightened up, he said. "Since my youth until this age of sixty-nine years (the next to the last year of his life) I

Qiu, have studied ceaselessly without having been taught the supreme science (Daoism). Now that the opportunity has come, judge the avidity with which I am going to listen to you." The old man said: "I don't know if we shall understand one another, for the common lot is that only persons with similar sentiments can understand each other. In any case, and with much risk, I am going to tell you my principles, and apply them to your conduct. You occupy yourself exclusively with the affairs of men, the emperor, lords, officials, plebeians; they are your interests. Let's speak of them. You attempt to take these four categories to task, obliging them to behave well, the final result being a perfect order in which everyone will live happy and content. Can you really create a world without evil and troubles? It is enough to afflict the plebeian that his field gives no harvest, his roof leaks, he lacks food or clothing, they impose a new tax on him, the women of the house argue or the young lack respect for their elders. Do you really intend to do away with all these things? The officials are sad because of the difficulties of their tasks, their failures, the negligence of their insubordinates, of the fact that their merits are not recognized and that they are not promoted. Can you really change all that? The lords complain of the disloyalty of their officials, the rebellions of their subjects, the clumsiness of their artisans, the poor quality of the rents that are paid to them in kind, the obligation to appear often at court with their hands full, and of the fact that the emperor is not satisfied with their presents. Can you do away with all that? The emperor is afflicted by disorders in the yin and the yang, heat and cold, which upset crop production and cause the people to suffer. He is afflicted by the quarrels and wars of his feudal lords which cost many men their lives. He is afflicted because his rules on rites and music are badly observed, his funds are used up, relationships are badly respected and the people behave badly. How can you suppress all these disorders? Have you the quality; have you the power, for that? You who are neither emperor, nor lord, nor even a minister, a simple private person; you claim to reform humanity. Isn't this trying to do more than you are capable of? Before seeing the realization of your dream, you must first of all deliver men from the eight manias I am going to enumerate for you: The mania to interfere in what is not one's business; the mania to speak without prior consideration; to lie, flatter, denigrate, sow discord, make a false impression on one's friends; and the mania to intrigue and insinuate. Are you the one who can make all these vices disappear? And the four following abuses; desire to innovate in order to make oneself famous; usurpation of the merit of others in order to promote oneself; obstinacy in one's faults despite remonstrations; obstinacy in one's ideas despite warnings. Can you change all that? If you can do that, then you can begin to expound your theories on goodness and fairness to people, with some chance that they will understand something." His face changed, and sighing with emotion, Confucius bowed down as thanks for the lesson, got up and said: "I admit that I am a utopian but I am not an evildoer. Why is it that I am honoured everywhere and then persecuted and expelled? What is it that attracts these ills to me? I don't understand it." "You don't understand!" said the old man, astonished, "truly you are a most limited man. It is your mania to occupy yourself with all and everything, to pose as censor and universal magistrate which attracts these tribulations to you. Listen to this story: A man was afraid of his shadow and footprints. To save himself he started to run. Now the more steps he took the more footprints he left. No matter how quickly he ran, his shadow did not leave him. Persisting despite all, thinking he would succeed through gaining speed, he ran so fast that he dropped dead. The imbecile; if he had sat down in the shade his body would no longer have cast a shadow; if he had kept still, his feet would have produced no footprints; he only had to keep himself in peace and all his ills would have disappeared. And you who, instead of keeping yourself in peace, make a profession of quibbling about goodness and fairness and I don't know what idle subtleties; you are astonished by the consequence of this mania. You don't understand that it is through irritating everyone that you have drawn universal hatred on yourself? Believe me, from the day when you no longer occupy yourself with yourself, and apply yourself to the cultivation of your natural basis, from the day when, returning to others what should be returned to them, you leave them in peace; that will be the day when you will no longer have any worries. It is through closing your eyes to yourself and opening them too much to others that you have attracted misfortune." All undone, Confucius asked: "What is my natural basis?" "One's natural basis," said the old man, "is the simplicity, sincerity, and uprightness that each one has at birth; that alone influences men. No one is touched by a false verbosity, by tears, shouts, or the pathos of a comedian. On the other hand true sentiments communicate themselves to others without the artifice of words or gestures. It is because they come from the natural basis, from native truth All true virtues are born from this basis, the affection of parents and the piety of children, loyalty towards ones prince, infectious joy at festivals and sincere passion at funerals. These sentiments are spontaneous and have nothing artificial about them whereas the rites in which you try to enmesh all the acts of life are a factitious comedy. The natural basis is the part each man has received from universal nature. Its dictum is invariable. It is the unique rule of conduct of the sage who scorns all human influence. Imbeciles do the opposite; they draw nothing from their own basis and are at the mercy of the influence of others. They do not know how to esteem the truth that is within them, but share in the frivolous and whimsical affections of the common people. It is a pity, Master, that you have spent all your life in untruth, and have only heard the truth expounded so lately." Confucius prostrated himself, got up, saluted and said: "What fortune that I have met you! What favour from heaven! Ah, Master, do not judge me unworthy to become your servant so that by serving you I may have the opportunity of learning more. Please tell me where you live. I will come to live with you in order to receive your teaching." "No!" said the old man. "The saying goes: Only reveal the mysteries to one who is capable of following you; don't reveal them to one who is incapable of understanding them. Your prejudices are too ingrained to be curable. Seek elsewhere, I am leaving you;" and saying that, the old man pushed on his gaff and disappeared with his boat amongst the green reeds. Although Yen Yuan had prepared the chariot for the return journey, and Zi Lu was holding the reins ready, Confucius could not tear himself away from the bank. At last, when the wash from the boat had entirely disappeared, and no more sound from the gaff reached his ears, he decided, with regret, to take his place in the chariot. Zi Lu, who walked alongside, said to him. "Master, I have now served you a long time. I have never seen you show so much respect and deference to anyone at all. Received by princes and lords and treated by them as an equal, you have always been haughty and disdainful. And today, in front of that old man leaning on his gaff, you bowed down at a right angle to listen to him and prostrated yourself before replying to him. Aren't these marks of veneration somewhat excessive? We disciples are surprised by them. On what grounds was this old fisherman worthy of such a fuss?" Leaning on the handrail, Confucius sighed and said: "Lu, you are decidedly incorrigible; my teaching slides without effect over your thick skull. Come closer and listen! Not to venerate an old man is to be lacking in the Rites. Not to honour a sage is to lack judgment. Not to bow before the virtue which shines in another is to do ill to oneself. Remember that, dolt! And if that is true of all virtue, how much more is it true of the science of Dao the Principle, through which all that is subsists, knowledge of which is life and ignorance of which is death. Conforming to the Principle gives success, opposing it is certain ruin. It is a sage's duty to honour the knowledge of the Principle wherever he finds it. Now this old fisherman possesses it. How could I not have honoured him as I did?" (Zhuang Zi, chapter 31)

Politicians; Confucius and the brigand Zhi.

Confucius was a friend of Ji of Liu Xia, who had a younger brother known as the Brigand Zhi. This individual had organized an association of nine thousand partizans who did whatever they pleased in the empire, holding princes to ransom, pillaging private property, rustling, kidnapping women and girls, not even sparing their own close relatives, and pushing impiety as far as not making offerings to their ancestors. As soon as they showed themselves, towns put themselves in a state of defence, and villagers entrenched themselves. Everyone had to suffer from these evildoers. Confucius said to Liuxia Ji: "Fathers should take their sons to task, older brothers their younger brothers. If they do not, it is because they do not take their responsibilities to heart. You are one of the finest officers of these times, and your younger brother is the Brigand Zhi. This man is the scourge of the empire, and you do not take him to task. I am warning you that I am going to give him a sermon in your place." Liuxia Ji said: "It is true that fathers and older brothers should take their sons and younger brothers to task, but when the sons and younger brothers refuse to listen, even if the father or older brother were as good at talking as you are, the result would be nil. Now my younger brother Zhi is a natural hothead with a fiery temper. On top of that he is so strong that he need fear no one, and he is so eloquent that he knows how to make his evil deeds appear good. He only likes those who flatter him, he goes into a rage when anyone contradicts him, and he does not hold himself back from violence. Believe me, keep away from him." Confucius did not heed this warning. He set out, Yen Hui driving the chariot and Zi Gong acting as counterweight. He found Zhi established at the south of Mount Shu, his band chopping up human livers for his dinner. Getting out of his chariot, Confucius went forward alone as far as the guard and said to him: "I, Kong Qiu of Lu, have heard tell of the elevated sentiments of your general; I wish to speak with him." And having said this, he saluted the guard with respect. The latter went away to notify the Brigand Zhi who became furious with the news to the point where his eyes shone like stars and his hair stood on end, lifting his bonnet. "This Kong Qiu," he said, "isn't he the sweet-talker of Lu? Tell him that he is a driveller who credits his rubbish to King Wen and Emperor Wu, who wears a hat of floral designs and a leather belt, who utters as many stupidities as words, who eats without working and clothes himself without spinning, who pretends it is enough for him to open his mouth and speak a few words for the distinction between good and evil to be established, who has led all the princes and learned astray, who, under cover of preaching piety, sucks up to the strong, noble and rich. Tell him he is the worst of evildoers and to clear off quickly or I will have his liver added to the stew which is being prepared for our dinner." The guard reported these words to Confucius, who still insisted and told him to say to Zhi that he wished to be received in his tent as a friend of his brother. The guard notified Zhi, who said: "Let him come." Confucius did not wait to be asked twice. He came forward quickly and went towards Zhi saluting. Full of rage, Zhi stretched out his two legs, placed his sword across them, fixed his eyes on Confucius, and with the tone of a tigress upset whilst feeding her young, he said: "Take care, Qiu! If you say things that please me, you will live! If you say anything whatever that displeases me, you will die!" Confucius said: "Three qualities are above all prized by men; a good bearing, great intelligence and military ability. Whoever possesses any one of these qualities in an eminent degree is fit to command men. Now, general, I see that you possess eminently all three of them. You are eight feet two inches tall, your eyes shine, your lips are red, your teeth are like white cowries, your voice rings like the sound of a bell; and a man who brings together all these qualities is called the Brigand Zhi! General, although I am unworthy of it, if you will take me as your counsellor I will use my credit to gain you the favour of all the neighbouring princes; I will have a great city built to be your capital; I will bring together hundreds of thousands of men to be your subjects; I will see that you become a strong and respected feudal prince. General, believe me, give the empire back its life; cease making war, and disband your soldiers so that families may live in peace on their subsistence and make offerings to their ancestors. Follow my advice, and you will acquire the reputation of being wise and brave; all the empire will applaud you." Still furious, Zhi replied: "Come off it, Qiu! You should know that you can only make a monkey out of a fool. Do I need you to teach me that the body my parents gave me is well made? Do you believe that your compliments touch me; I who know that you run me down elsewhere more than you have flattered me here? And then, the chimerical blow with which you try to take me, it's really too crude. But supposing that I obtained what you promised me, how long would I keep it? Has the empire not escaped from the descendants of Yao and Shun; aren't the posterity of Emperors Tang and Wu extinct, precisely because their ancestors left them a very rich patrimony which was much sought-after? Power does not last, and happiness does not consist, as you and like politicians would have us believe, in these things. In the beginning there were many animals and few people. During the day the latter collected acorns and chestnuts; during the night they sought refuge in the trees out of fear of wild animals. This was called the nest period. Then came the age of the caves during which men, still naked, collected fuel in summer to keep them warm in winter; the first manifestation of care for the maintenance of human life. Then came the age of Shen Nong, the first agriculturalist; an absolutely carefree age. Men only knew their mother, not their father (there was no marriage). They lived in peace with the elk and the deer. They cultivated sufficient to eat, and spun enough to clothe themselves. No one wronged another. That was the time when everything followed its natural course, in perfection. The Yellow Emperor put an end to this happy age. He assumed imperial power and was the first to make war. He went into battle at Zhou Lu where he spilt blood over an area of one hundred stages by pursuing those he had defeated. Then Yao and Shun invented ministers of state and thc administrative machinery. Then Tang re-volted and exiled his sovereign Jie; Wu dethroned and executed Emperor Zhou. From that time until our days, the strong have oppressed the weak and the majority have tyrannized the minority. All the emperors and princes have troubled the world, just like the first of their kind. And you, Qiu, have given yourself the mission of propagating the principles of King Wen and Emperor Wu, and you aspire to impose these principles on posterity. It is with this claim that you wear a hat and belt different to those worn by the people; that you hold forth in speech, and pose, duping princes and pushing your own interests. You are without contradiction the worst amongst evil-doers, and in place of calling me pre-eminently the Brigand Zhi, the people should call you the Brigand Qiu. I will recall the, results of your teaching for you. After having bamboozled Zi Lu, you made him disarm and study. The astonished world said Qiu knows how to soften the violent; but the illusion did not last. Having tried to assassinate the Prince of Wei, Zi Lu perished, and his salted body (salted so that it would last longer) was exposed at the eastern gate of the capital of Wei. Should I continue to enumerate the successes of the man of talent, the great sage you think yourself to be? They got rid of you twice from Lu. You were expelled from Wei. At Qi you almost had real trouble. You were under siege between Chen and Cai. The whole empire refused to give asylum to the master who had loused up his disciple, Zi Lu. In summary, you have not been of use to yourself nor to others, and yet you claim that one should hold your doctrine in esteem. 'This doctrine,' you say, 'is not my doctrine. It goes back via the ancient sovereigns as far as the Yellow Emperor.' Only the common people can be deceived by these famous paragons. Unleashing his wild passions, the Yellow Emperor made the first war and spilt blood on the Plain of Zhou Lu. Yao was a bad father. Shun was a bad son. Yu stole the empire in order to give it to his family (he made it hereditary). Tang banished his sovereign. Wu killed his sovereign. King Wen put You Li in prison. There you have the six paragons, the admiration of whom you impose on the common people. Considered closely, they were men whose love of their own interests made them act against their consciences and against nature; men whose acts are worthy of profound contempt. And the other great men, did they not all perish victims of their own stupidity? Their utopias were the cause of Bo Yi and Shu Qi dying of starvation and remaining without burial. Bao Jaio's ideal was the cause of his retiring to the forest where he was found dead on his knees embracing a tree-trunk. His spite at not being listened to, caused Shen Tu Di to tie a rock on his back and jump in the river, where the fish and turtles ate him. The faithful Jie Zi Tui who went so far as to nourish his Duke Wen with a piece of his thigh, was so upset by the ingratitude of the latter that he withdrew himself into the forest where he perished in a fire. Wei Shang who had arranged a rendezvous with a beauty under a bridge, allowed himself to be drowned by the rising waters rather than fail to keep his word to her. In what, I ask you, does the lot of these six men differ from that of a crushed dog, a pig whose throat is cut, or a beggar dead from starvation? Their passions caused their death. They would have done better to have maintained their lives in peace. Again you give as examples faithful ministers such as Bai Gan and Wu Zixu. Now Bai Gan was put to death and his heart was torn out. Wu Zixu had to commit suicide and his body was thrown into the river. There you can see what their faithfulness was worth to them, to become a public laughing-stock. Therefore, of every true to life example you quote as proof of your system, not one convinces me but quite the opposite. If then you should put forward arguments from beyond the grave, I can tell you that such things mean nothing to me. For my part, I am going to give you a practical lesson on what humanity really is. Man likes the satisfaction of his eyes, ears, mouth, and instincts. He has but the duration of his life in which to satisfy his inclinations, an average of sixty years, sometimes eighty, and rarely a hundred. Yet one must subtract from these years the periods of illness, sadness and misfortunes, so much that in a month of life a man has scarcely four or five days of real contentment and frank laughter. The course of time is infinite, but the lot of life assigned to each one is finite, and death puts an end to it in its time. An existence is only, in the succession of the centuries, like the leap of a horse across a ditch. Now in my opinion he who does not know how to make his short life last as long as possible, and does not, during that time, satisfy all the inclinations of his nature, understands nothing of what humanity really is. In conclusion, Qiu, I deny all that you affirm, and I uphold everything you deny. Take care not to reply a single word. Clear off quickly; fool, braggart, utopian, liar; you have nothing of what it takes to put men back on their road. I shall say nothing more to you." Confucius saluted humbly and left in haste. When he came to climb into his chariot, he was so flustered that he had to try three times before he could find and grip the handrail. With no lustre in his eyes, his face livid, he leant on the handrail, his head bowed, gasping for breath. As he was entering the town by the eastern gate he met Liuxia Ji. "Ah, there you are!" said the latter. "It is some time since I saw you. You look weary. You haven't by any chance been to see Zhi?" "I have!" said Confucius, raising his eyes to heaven and sighing deeply. "And has he allowed a single one of the things you said to him," asked Liuxia Ji. "He hasn't agreed with any of it," said Confucius. "You were right. This time I have done like the man who cauterized himself when he was not ill. I have tugged on the tigers whiskers, and been lucky to escape its teeth." (Zhuang Zi, chapter 29).

Geng Sang Chu.

Among the followers of Lao Dan (the posthumous name of Lao Zi), a certain Geng Sang Chu went north, established himself at the foot of Mount Wei Lei, and taught disciples in his turn. For the love of Daoist simplicity, he dismissed those of his servants who gave themselves intelligent airs, and kept away from those of his concubines who were refined, only keeping rustic and weather beaten types around himself. Three years later, through the effect of his presence and example, Wei Lei found prosperity. The people of the place said to one another "When Master Geng Sang Chu established himself amongst us, we found it strange. That was because we did not know him well enough; now that we have had time to get to know him, who amongst us does not consider him a sage? Why don't we make him our local sage, honouring him as one does the representative of the dead, the genie of the sun and the one of the harvests, by reverence and offerings at certain times of the year?" Geng Sang Chu learnt of these proposals. Seated in his school, in his position of master, he looked embarrassed. His disciples asked him why. "Because," he said, "according to my master Lao Dan, if the spring brings the plants back to life and autumn makes the fruits ripen, these are natural effects produced by Dao, the great Principle, operating in everything, and not from the merits of the seasons. Just like nature, the superior man should remain hidden (inside his house) and not allow the crowds to acclaim him. Now it happens that these little people of Wei Lei are thinking of giving me the rank and offerings of a sage. This embarrasses me, for I do not wish to contravene the teaching of my master Lao Dan." "Have no fear," said the disciples; "you have the qualities, and the position is easy. A whale cannot turn round in a canal, but a small fish moves in it with ease. A buffalo would not be safe on a knoll, but a fox would live there quite well. And then, why shouldn't sages be honoured, the able elevated, the good and useful distinguished? This has been the general rule since the days of Yao and Shun. Master, let these little people of Wei Lei do as they wish. Give in to their wishes." Geng Sang Chu said: "Approach, my children so that I may explain to you. Showing oneself is always deadly. Even an animal large enough to swallow a carriage would not avoid nets and snares were it to leave its hide-out in the mountains. Even a fish big enough to swallow a boat would be eaten by the ants if it were stranded. It is for their own safety that birds and wild beasts seek the high places, fish and turtles the deep waters. In the same way, he who wishes to protect himself should hide away in retreat and mystery. As for Yao and Shun, whom you have cited, their authority is null. What have they done for the good of humanity, these phrase-coiners, innovators, thinkers wholly occupied with vulgarities and trifles? They honoured the learned, the finest way to make the people competitive. They elevated the skilled and the able; the best way to make everyone brigands. Of all their inventions, none have given benefit to the people. Quite the contrary, they over-excited the people to egoism, a passion which makes parricides, regicides, thieves and pillagers. I tell you, all the disorders date from the reigns of these two men. If their politics are continued, a day will come when men will devour one another."

Nan Rong Zhu (a man already advanced in years, who had put himself in the school of Geng Sang Chu) assumed the most respectful posture, and said to him: "At my age, what can I do to become a superior man?" Geng Sang Chu said: "See to it that your healthy body imprisons your vital spirit completely; do not let thoughts or images buzz inside you; if you do that for three whole years, you will obtain what you desire." Nan Rong Zhu replied: "All eyes appear alike, but those of the blind do not see. All ears appear the same, but those of the deaf do not hear. All hearts appear the same, and yet fools do not understand. In my body, I am made like you, but my mind must differ from yours. I cannot grasp the meaning of your words." "That must be due to my incapacity to explain myself," said Geng Sang Chu. "A little fly can do nothing for a big sphinx. A little hen from Yue cannot incubate a goose egg. Evidently I have not the ability to teach you the Way. Why don't you go south and consult Lao Zi?"

Following Geng Sang Chu's advice, Nan Rong Zhu furnished himself with the necessary provisions, walked for seven days and nights, and reached the place where Lao Zi lived. "Did Geng Sang Chu send you," asked the latter. "Yes," said Nan Rong Zhu. "Why have you brought such a large retinue" (of prejudices, attachments, illusions, and errors) asked Lao Zi. Nan Rong Zhu looked behind himself quite scared. "You did not understand my question," said Lao Zi. Nan Rong Zhu lowered his head in shame, then, having raised it, he sighed and said: "Because I could not understand your question, do you forbid me to say what has brought me here?" "No," said Lao Zi, "go on." Then Nan Rong Zhu said: "If I stay ignorant, people will scoff at me; if I become learned, it will have worn me out. If I stay bad, I will do evil to others; if I become good, it will wear me out. If I do not practise fairness, I shall wound others; if I practise it, I shall harm myself. These three doubts torment me. What should I do, or not do? Geng Sang Chu has sent me to ask your advice." Lao Zi said: "At the first glance I saw clearly in your eyes that you had lost your head. You are like a man who tries to recover his drowned parents from the bottom of the sea. I pity you." Nan Rong Zhu was admitted to Lao Zi's household as a paying guest, and began a moral treatment. He applied himself first of all to fixing his qualities and eliminating his vices. After ten days of this exercise, which was hard for him, he saw Lao Zi again, who said: "Is the work of your purification advancing? It seems to me that it is not yet perfect. Troubles from outside (entered through the senses) can only be stopped by the opposition of an internal barrier (withdrawal). Those from within (coming from the mind) can only be barred by an external barrier (self-control). Even those who are advanced in the science of the Principle occasionally experience attacks from these two kinds of emotions, and still have to guard themselves against them; how much more so those like you who have lived a long time without knowing the Principle and are little advanced." "Alas!" said Nan Rong Zhu, discouraged, "when a peasant falls ill he blames his illness on another, and finds himself at least relieved, if not cured. Whereas each time I consult on the great Principle, the ill that torments my heart increases, as though I had taken the wrong medicine. It is too much for me. Please give me the recipe to prolong my life; that will be enough for me." "And you think" said Lao Zi, "that it can be passed on just like that, from hand to hand? Prolonging life assumes many things. Are you capable of conserving your physical integrity, of not compromising it? Would you always be able to distinguish the favourable from the fatal? Would you be able to stop yourself, and abstain yourself, to the limit? Could you become disinterested in others in order to become concentrated in your own interior? Could you come to keep your mind free and withdrawn? Could you return to the state of your first infancy? The new-born baby cries day and night without becoming hoarse, so solid is its nature. It does not let go of what it grasps, so concentrated is its will. It looks at length without blinking, nothing moving it. It moves without aim and stops without motive, spontaneously, without reflection. Being indifferent and following nature is the formula for prolonging life." "All the formula?" asked Nan Rong Zhu. Lao Zi went on: "That is just the beginning, what I call the thawing out, the breaking up of the ice, after which the river begins to take its course. The superior man lives like other men on the fruits of the earth, the gifts of good things from heaven. But he is attached neither to people nor to things. Profit and loss leave him equally indifferent. Nothing offends him; nothing makes him rejoice. He glides, concentrated in himself. This is the formula for making one's life last." "All the formula?" asked Nan Rong Zhu again. Lao Zi continued: "I have said that one must become again like a little child. Moving, acting, the child has no aim, no intention. His body is indifferent like dead wood; his heart is inert like cold ashes. For him there is neither happiness nor sadness. What harm can men do to one who is above these two great vicissitudes of destiny? The superior being is one who is lodged in indifference." (Zhuang Zi, ch. 23).

The soothsayer cannot see everything clearly.

Zi Qi had eight sons. He lined them up in front of the physiognomist Jiu Fang Yin, and said to him: "Please examine these boys and tell me which one shows signs of good fortune." The soothsayer said: "This one, Kun." Surprised and full of joy, the father said: "What do you predict for him?" "He will eat the food of a prince until the end of his days," said the soothsayer. With these words, Zi Qi's happiness turned to sadness. He said weeping: "What evil has my son done that he should have such a destiny." "What do you mean," said the soothsayer. "When someone eats at a prince's table, this honour resounds as far as the third generation of his ancestry. You will therefore have your share of your son's good fortune. And you weep as if you were afraid of this good luck; how could something fortunate for your son be unfortunate for you." "Alas," said Zi Qi, "are you quite sure that you interpret my son's destiny correctly, that he will have wine and meat at his pleasure all his life? This is a good thing, no doubt; but what price will he pay for it? That is what you have perhaps not seen clearly. I distrust this presage because nothing but extraordinary things happen to me. Although I don't keep sheep, a ewe has come to drop her lambs in my house. Although I do not hunt, a quail has made her nest there. Are these not strange happenings? I have a great fear that my son also will have a strange future. I would have wished him to live always as I do, free between heaven and earth, enjoying like me the good things of heaven and earth and eating the fruits of the earth. I do not wish him any more than myself to have worries, concerns or adventures. I wish him, like myself, to climb so high in natural simplicity that no earthly thing can impress him any more. I would have wished that, like me, he would have become absorbed in indifference, not in interest. And here you are, predicting one of the most vulgar rewards. This implies that he will have rendered the most vulgar service. The presage is therefore ill-omened. It is probably an inevitable fatality, for neither my son nor I have sinned, so this must be a decree of destiny. That is why I weep." Later, both the soothsayer's prediction and the father's apprehension were realized in the following way: Zi Qi sent his son Kun to the land of Yen. On the way he was seized by brigands. Seeing that it would be hard to sell him entire as a slave, they cut off one of his feet and then sold him in the Principality of Qi where he became inspector of the refuse dump in the capital. Until the end of his life he ate his share of the Prince of Qi's left-overs, just as the soothsayer had predicted, a prey to the vilest of worries, just as his father had predicted. (Zhuang Zi, chapter 24).

The seer duped.

One of the most transcendent seers, Ji Xian, from the Principality of Qi, established himself in Zheng. He predicted illness and death to the exact day, infallibly. Therefore the people of Zheng who could not bear to know these things so long in advance, ran away whenever they saw him coming. Lie Zi went to see him and marvelled at what he saw and heard. When he returned to his master, Hu Zi, he said: "Until now I held your doctrine to be the most perfect, but now I have found a better one." Hu Zi said: "That is because you do not know all of my doctrine. I have only given you the exoteric teaching, and not the esoteric. Your knowledge is like those eggs laid by hens with no cock; it lacks the essential (the germ). Moreover, when one argues, one must have a firm faith on one's opinion. If one should waver, there is a risk of being divined by the adversary. This could be what has happened to you. You could have been deceived, and then taken the natural flair of Ji Xian as transcendent divination. Bring this man to me so that I may see what it is all about." The next day Lie Zi brought the seer to Hu Zi under pretext of a medical consultation. When he came out, the seer said to Lie Zi: "Alas, your master is a dead man. He will be gone within a few days. On examining him I had a strange vision, as of humid ashes, an omen of death." When he had sent the seer away, Lie Zi went in shedding tears and reported the prognosis to Hu Zi. The latter said: "I manifested myself to him as an inert and sterile earth, with all my energy arrested, (an aspect that common people show only on the approach of death, but which the contemplative can produce at will). He has been taken in by it. Bring him again, and you will see the next stage of the experiment." The next day, Lie Zi brought back the seer. When he came out, the seer said to Lie Zi: "Your master has done well by addressing himself to me; there is already an improvement; the ashes are becoming re-animated; I have seen signs of vital energy." Lie Zi reported these words to Hu Zi, who said: "That is because I manifested myself to him as an earth fecundated by heaven, with energy rising from the depths under an influence from above. He has seen clearly, but he has interpreted it wrongly, (taking what has resulted from my concentration as natural). Bring him again, so that we may continue the experiment." The next day Lie Zi brought the seer. After his examination, he said: "Today I have found a vague and indeterminate aspect in your master. I cannot make any prognosis from this, but when his condition becomes more clearly defined I will be able to tell you what it is." Lie Zi reported these words to Hu Zi, who said: "That is because I manifested myself to him under the form of a great chaos, as yet undifferentiated, all my forces being in a state of neutral equilibrium. He could in fact draw nothing clear from this. A swell in the water can be caused just as well by a sea monster, a reef, the strength of the current, a spring, a cascade, the meeting of two currents of water, a dam, a deflection, or by the breaching of a dyke; an identical effect produced by nine different causes. (It is therefore impossible to conclude the nature of its cause directly from the swell; further examination is necessary to determine the latter). Bring him once more, and you will see the sequel." The next day the seer stopped for only an instant in front of Hu Zi, understood nothing, lost his composure, and fled. "Run after him!" said Hu Zi. Lie Zi obeyed but could not catch up with him. "He will not come back," said Hu Zi. "I manifested myself to him as coming from the Primordial Principle before time, a movement in the void without apparent form, a boiling of inert force. It was too much for him, that's why he has taken to flight." Realising that in fact he still understood nothing of his master's esoteric doctrine, Lie Zi stayed at home for three whole years. He did the cooking for his wife, and served the pigs as though they were people (in order to destroy any human prejudices within him). He cut himself off from outside interests and he brought his own artificial culture back to a primitive natural simplicity. He became like a lump of earth, a stranger to all events and happenings, and thus he remained, concentrated on unity, until the end of his days. (Lie Zi, ch. 2).

Hunting grasshoppers.

When Confucius was travelling in the Kingdom of Chu, coming out of a wood he saw a hunchback who was catching flying grasshoppers with a rod, just as easily as one picks up an object with the hand. 'You are truly skilled,' said Confucius to him; 'tell me your secret.' 'My secret is this,' said the hunchback: 'For about six months I practised holding balls steady on the end of my rod. When I could hold two, few grasshoppers escaped me. When I could hold three, I missed only one in ten. When I could hold five, I never missed any. My secret consists in concentrating all my energy on the goal. I have mastered my arm, my entire body, such that they show no more emotion or distraction than a piece of wood. In the vast universe full of things, I see only the grasshopper that I wish to take. Since nothing distracts me, it is taken naturally.' Turning himself towards his disciples, Confucius said to them: 'To unify one's intentions; to have only one, which becomes blended with the vital energy; that sums up this hunchback's discourse.' (The commentators explain this in two ways. He stabbed them in flight, say some; hardly believable. There was glue on the end of the rod, say others; most likely). (Zhuang Zi, chapter 19).

The beautiful and the ugly.

When Yang Zhu was passing through the Principality of Song he stayed in a hostel where the host had two wives, one beautiful, the other ugly. The ugly one was liked, the beauty was detested... "Why so?" asked Yang Zhu of a little servant; "Because," said the child, "the beautiful one shows off her beauty, which makes her unpleasant to us; whereas the ugly one knows that she is ugly, which makes us forget her ugliness." "Remember that," said Yang Zhu to his followers. "Being wise, do not pose as having wisdom; that is the secret of being liked everywhere." (Lie Zi, ch. 2).

The monkey keeper.

A monkey keeper of the Principality of Song came to understand monkeys and to communicate with them. He treated them better than the members of his family, refusing them nothing. However, he fell into dire straits. Obliged to ration his monkeys, he thought up the following means of persuasion. From now on," he said to them, "you will each have three taro roots in the morning, and four in the evening. Will that be all right?" All the monkeys were furious. Then he said, "how about four taros in the morning and three in the evening; will that suit you?" Satisfied that he had taken notice of their displeasure, the monkeys all settled down quite content. That is how one wins over the animals. The sage likewise wins over foolish humans. The means employed matter little, be they real or apparent, provided that they satisfy, and do not irritate. (Lie Zi, chapter 2).

Meeting of Lao Zi with Yang Zhu.

Yang Zhu was going to Pei and Lao Zi was going to Qin. The two met each other at Liang. On seeing Yang Zhu, Lao Zi raised his eyes to heaven, and said with a sigh: "I had hoped to be able to teach you, but I see there is no way." Yang Zhu did not reply. When the two travellers reached the hostel where they spent the night, Yang Zhu himself brought all the things required for the toilet. Then, when Lao Zi was settled in his room, Yang Zhu left his shoes by the door and went in on his knees, and said: "I did not understand what you said about me when you raised your eyes to heaven and sighed. I did not ask you for an explanation then, as I did not wish to delay your journey. But now that you are free, please explain the meaning of your words to me." "You have a haughty look which rebuffs" said Lao Zi; "whereas the sage appears confused even though he is irreproachable. He considers himself inadequate, whatever his state of perfection." "I will benefit from your lesson," said Yang Zhu, rooted to the spot with shock. Even that same night Yang Zhu humbled himself so much that the staff of the inn, who had served him with so much respect on his arrival, paid no attention to him on the morning of his departure. (The respect of servants in China is proportional to the haughtiness of the traveller). (Lie Zi, chapter 2).

Dreams; the butterfly.

(There are no real individuals as such, but only prolongations of the norm:) "Once," relates Zhuang Zi, "one night, I was a butterfly flitting about contented with its lot. Then I woke up as Zhuang Zi. Who am I in reality? A butterfly who dreams he is Zhuang Zi, or Zhuang Zi who dreamt he was a butterfly? In my case, are there two individuals? Has there been a real transformation of one individual into another?" (Neither one nor the other, says the commentary. There have been two unreal modifications of the unique being, the universal norm, in which all beings in all their states are one). (Zhuang Zi, ch. 2).

Dreams; the rich man and his valet.

A certain Yin, an official of the Zhou dynasty, lived in luxury. His servants got no rest from dawn till night. An old valet, broken and feeble, was no less abused than the others. Now, after having suffered hardship all day, each night the man dreamt he was a prince, seated on a throne, governing a country, and enjoying all the pleasures of it. On awaking he found himself once more a valet, and suffered as such the whole day through. When his friends complained of their lot, the old valet said to them: "I am not so given to complaining. Life is equally divided into day and night. During the day I am a valet and suffer, but during the night I am a prince and enjoy myself very much. It is good half of the time; why should I complain?" However the master of this valet, after a day of pleasure dreamt each night that he was a valet, bowed down with worry, snarled at and rebuked. He told a friend of this. The latter said to him: "It must be because during the day you have exceeded the lot of pleasure assigned to you by destiny. Destiny compensates for this by your suffering at night." The official believed his friend, moderated his luxury, treated his servants better, and found himself the better for it. (Straight away the old valet lost his nocturnal pleasure which destiny had allowed him in compensation for the excess of his daily fatigues). (Lie Zi, chapter 3).

Dreams; the clairvoyant turtle.

One night, in a dream, Prince Yuan of Song saw a weeping human figure at the door of his bedchamber, and it said to him: "I come from the Zai Lu chasm. The Genie of Ceng Jiang had deputized me to the one of the Yellow River. On my way there, I was taken by Yu Ju the fisherman." On awaking, Prince Yuan ordered his seers to interpret his dream. They replied: "The being you saw is a transcendent turtle." The prince asked: "Is there, among the fishermen here, one called Yu Ju?" "Yes", said his assistants. "See to it that he appears before me," said the prince. The next day, at the official audience, the fisherman presented himself. "What have you caught," the prince asked him. "I found a white turtle in my net, five feet in circumference," said the fisherman. "Give it to me," ordered the prince. When it had been brought, the prince asked himself if he should have it killed or if he should save its life. He asked the Fates for the solution to his doubt. The reply was: "To kill the turtle would be advantageous for divination." The turtle was therefore killed. Its carapace was perforated in seventy-two places. Not one of these divinations gave a false answer. Confucius heard about this and said: "Thus this transcendent turtle could appear afterwards to Prince Yuan, but could not foresee and avoid its own capture. After its death its carapace continued to make infallible predictions for others, but it had been unable to predict its own death. It is clear that science has its limits and that transcendence itself does not extend to everything." (Zhuang Zi, ch. 26).

The roebuck killed in a dream.

A butcher from Zheng, who was collecting firewood, came across a stray roebuck which he killed and hid under some branches in a hollow, intending to remove it in secret later. On returning, he could not find the place, and believing that he had dreamt it he told the story to others. One of his listeners, following his directions, found the roebuck and brought it home. "This butcher's dream was real," said the people of his house. "Real for you," they said, "since it is you who found the roebuck." However the next night the butcher had a revelation in a dream that such a person had found his roebuck and hidden it in his house. He went there early in the morning, discovered the roebuck, and accused the person before the village chief. The latter said to the butcher: "If you killed the roebuck whilst awake, why did you tell the story that you did it in a dream? If you killed the roebuck in a dream, it could not be this real roebuck. Therefore, since it cannot be ascertained that you killed the beast, I cannot give judgment in your favour. Moreover, since your adversary found it from directions given in your dream, and you found it again after another dream, you should divide it between the two of you." The village chief's judgment was brought to the attention of the Prince of Zheng, who asked his minister what he thought about it. The minister said: "In order to decide what is and what is not a dream, and to decide legal rights in a matter of dreams, only the Yellow Emperor and Confucius are qualified. Since we have neither of them to settle this litigation, I think we should stick to the arbitrary judgment of the village chief." (Lie Zi, chapter 3).

A hidden sage; the counterbalanced ladle.

Zi Gong, a disciple of Confucius, had been to the Principality of Chu and was coming back towards that of Jin. Near the Han River he saw a man busy watering his vegetable garden. He filled a container at the well and subsequently emptied it into the troughs of his beds of plants; it was hard work giving little result. "Don't you know," said Zi Gong, "that there is a machine with which a hundred beds are easily watered in a day without hard work." "How does it work?" asked the man. Zi Gong replied: "It is a counterbalanced ladle that takes the water from one side and pours it out at the other." "Too clever to be good!" said the gardener, annoyed. "I learnt from my master that all machines have to do with formulae, artificiality. Now formulae and artifices destroy native ingenuity, trouble the vital spirits and prevent the Principle from residing peacefully in one's heart. I want nothing of your counterbalanced ladle." Silenced, Zi Gong lowered his head, and did not reply. In his turn, the gardener asked: "Who are you?" "A Confucian," said Zi Gong. "Ah!" said the gardener. "One of those pedants who think they are superior to the common people and try to make themselves interesting by singing complaints about the bad state of the empire. Go! Forget your mind, forget your body, and you will take the first step along the road to wisdom. For, if you cannot put yourself aright, how can you claim to set aright the empire? Off you go now! You have made me waste enough time." Zi Gong went away pale with emotion. He did not recover until after he had covered thirty Li. Then the disciples who accompanied him, asked: "What kind of man is he, to have troubled you so?" "Ah!" said Zi Gong. "Until now I believed that there was in the empire but a single man worthy of his name, my master Confucius. That was because I did not know this man. I explained to him the Confucian theory of the tendency towards the goal by the most fitting means, and with the least effort. I took that for the formula of wisdom. Now he has refuted me, and given me to understand that wisdom consists of integration of the vital spirits, conservation of one's nature, and union with Dao the Principle. These true sages do not differ from the common people on the outside; inside, their distinctive trait is an absence of goal; letting life unfold without wanting to know where it is going. All effort, tendency, art, is for them the result of having forgotten what man should be. According to them the true man only moves under his natural instinct. He scorns praise and blame equally, which neither give him benefit nor deprive him. That is true wisdom, whereas I am buffeted about by the wind and the waves." When they got back to the Principality of Lu, Zi Gong, converted to Daoism, recounted his adventure to Confucius. The latter said: "This man claims to practise the wisdom of the primordial age. He holds himself to the principle, to the formula, affecting ignorance of applications and modifications. Certainly, if in the present world there were still a means of living without thinking and without acting, attending uniquely to one's own well-being, there would be grounds for admiring him. But we were born, you and I, in a century of intrigues and struggles where the wisdom of the primordial age is no longer worth studying for it is no longer applicable." (Zhuang Zi, chapter 12).

Life and death; the four friends.

Zi Si, Zi Yu, Zi Li and Zi Lai were talking. One of them said: "I will take as my friend he who thinks as I do that all beings are eternal, and life and death succeed one another as two phases of the same being." Now the three others thought the same, and all four men laughed and became close friends. Now it happened that Zi Yu fell seriously ill. He was horribly humpbacked and deformed. Zi Si went to see him. Breathing painfully but with a calm heart, the dying man said to him: "If when I have left this form, my left arm is made into a cock, I will sing to announce the dawn, if it is made into a bolt for a crossbow, I will knock down the crows. If my trunk is made into a carriage harnessed to my spirit transformed into a horse, I shall still be satisfied. Each being receives its form in its time, and leaves it at the appointed time, so why conceive of happiness and sadness in these vicissitudes? There is no place for it. As the ancients said, the faggot is successively bound and unbound. The being does not bind or unbind itself. It depends on heaven for life and death. Why should I, a being among beings, complain about dying?" Next, Zi Lai fell ill. He was gasping for breath and close to death. His wife and children were crying all around him. Zi Li went to visit him, and said to them: "Shut up! Get out! Don't trouble his passing" (which requires calm, just as going to sleep does). Then, leaning against the door-post, he said to the patient: "Transformation is good. What is it going to make of you? Where are you going? Will you become an organ of a rat or the foot of an insect?" "It matters little to me," said the dying man. "The child must go in whatever direction his parents send him. Now the yin and the yang are more to a man than his parents. When their revolution brings about my death, if I do not submit myself willingly, I shall be a rebel. The great mass (the cosmos) has served me for my living, consoled me in my old age and gives me peace in death. It has been good to me in life, and it will be so in death. Let us imagine a smelter melting his metal. If a bit of the metal, jumping up, were to say: 'I want to become a sword, no other thing,' it is quite likely that the smelter would find this metal unsuitable. Likewise if, at the time of transformation, a dying man were to cry out 'I want to become a man again, no other thing,' it is equally likely that the transformer would find him unsuitable. Heaven and earth (the cosmos) is the great furnace, transformation is the great smelter; whatever it should make of us should be agreeable to us. Let us abandon ourselves to it in peace. Life ends in a sleep which is followed by a new awakening." (Zhuang Zi, chapter 6).

Life and death; the funeral.

Master Sang Hu, Meng Zi Fan, and Master Qin Zhang were friends. One of them said: "Who is perfectly indifferent to any influence, to any action. Who can elevate himself to the heavens by abstraction, saunter on the clouds by speculation, play in the ether and forget the present life and the death to come?" The three men looked at each other and laughed, for they were all like that, and they became better friends than ever. When one of the three, Master Sang Hu, died, Confucius sent his disciple Zi Gong to the dead man's house to ask if assistance were needed for the funeral. When Zi Gong arrived, the two surviving friends were singing the following refrain in front of the corpse, accompanied by a lute: "O Sang Hu! O Sang Hu! There you are united with transcendence whereas we are still men, alas." Zi Gong went up to them and said: "Is it in conformity with the rites to sing like that in the presence of a corpse?" The two men looked at one another and burst out laughing, saying: "What can this guy understand of our rites?" Zi Gong went back and told Confucius what he had seen, and said to him: "What kind of men are these, with neither manners nor bearing, who sing in front of a corpse without any trace of sadness? I understand nothing of this." "These people move outside the world," said Confucius. "There can be nothing in common between us and them.

I was wrong to send you there. According to them, man should live in communion with the author of beings (the cosmic Principle), by placing himself at the time when heaven and earth were not yet separated. For them, the form they have in this existence is an accessory, an appendage of which death delivers them whilst waiting to be reborn in another. In consequence, for them, there is neither life nor death, past nor future in the usual meaning of these words. According to them the matter of their bodies has served, and will successively serve a number of different beings. Their viscera and organs are of little importance to people who believe in a continual succession of beginnings and endings. They walk in spirit outside this dusty world, and abstain from mixing in its affairs; why should they give themselves the trouble of accomplishing the common rites, or even the appearance of accomplishing them?" "But you, Master," said Zi Gong, won over to Daoism, "why do you make these rites the basis of your morality?" "Because heaven has condemned me to this irksome task," said Confucius. "I speak thus, but in fact like you I no longer believe in it. Fish are born in the water, people in the Principle. The true superior person is one who has broken with all the rest in order to adhere uniquely to heaven. None other should be called a sage. Too often those who are called sages are only common people in the eyes of heaven." (Zhuang Zi, ch. 6).

Karma; fate, destiny.

Bei Gong Zi said to Xi Men Zi: "I was born at the same time and come from the same lineage as you; there is scarcely any difference between our features, language, and bearing; however, you succeed, you are liked, relished, honoured and praised whereas quite the opposite happens to me. We have tried our fortune using the same means; you have succeeded in everything, I in nothing. I am badly clothed, fed, housed and walk on foot; whereas you live in luxury and abundance and only go out in a quadriga. And in your private as well as your public life you excel so much that I no longer dare compare myself with you." "I think," said Xi Men Zi, "that the difference in our condition comes from the difference in our conduct. You must behave less well than I do." Most humiliated, Bei Gong Zi did not know what to say, and went away quite nonplussed. In the street he met the Master of the Eastern Suburb who said to him: "Where are you going looking like that?" Bei Gong Zi told him of his perplexity. "Let's go back there together," said the Master. "I'll sort out this affront." When they reached Xi Men Zi's home, the Master said: "What did you tell Bei Gong Zi to upset him so?" "I told him that I thought the difference in our position had come from the difference in our behaviour," said Xi Men Zi. "Nothing of the kind," said the Master. "This is how it should be explained: Bei Gong Zi is well-gifted but has a bad destiny. You, Xi Men Z1, are badly-gifted but have a good destiny. Your success is not due to your qualities and his failures are not due to his inability. You have not made yourself what you are; it is fate that has done that. If therefore you, the fortunate one, have humiliated him; if he, the gifted one, has felt shame, it is because both of you are ignorant of what you are." "Say no more, Master!" said Xi Men Zi; "I will not act like that again." When Bei Gong Zi got home, he found his coarse robe warmer than a fox or badger fur; his coarse food seemed delicious; his hovel seemed like a palace and his screen a carriage. The light shone inside him and until his death he paid no further attention to social distinctions. The Master of the Eastern Suburb learnt of his changed attitude and said: "After a very long sleep (in ignorance), a word has been enough to wake this man, and change him in a lasting way." (Lie Zi, chapter 6).

Books; detritus of the ancients.

One day, whilst Duke Huan of Qi was reading, seated in the great hall, Pian the wheelwright was making a wheel in the courtyard. Suddenly, putting down his hammer and chisel, he climbed the stairs, approached the duke and said to him: "What are you reading there." "The words of the sages," replied the duke. "Of living sages?" asked Pian. "Of dead sages," said the duke. "Ah!" said Pian, "the rubbish of the ancients." Irritated, the duke said to him: "Wheelwright, what right have you to interfere? Explain yourself quickly or I will have you put to death." "I will explain as a man of my craft," replied the wheelwright. "When I make a wheel, if I go gently, the result is weak, if I go strongly the result is massive; if I go without thinking of what I am doing, the result conforms to my ideal of a good and beautiful wheel. I cannot define this method for it is a knack which cannot be explained, so much so that I have not been able to explain it to my son, and at the age of seventy, to have a good wheel I still have to make it myself. Were the ancient defunct sages, whose books you read, able to do better than I? Could they write down their knack, their genius? If not, their books contain only the refuse of their departed spirit." (Zhuang Zi, chapter 13).

Archery; the purpose of.

Lie Zi wished to learn archery, and asked Guan Yin Zi to teach him. The latter wanted to know if he knew the purpose of archery. "No!" said Lie Zi. "Then go and find out," said Guan Yin Zi, "and then come back." Three years later, Lie Zi went back. "Do you know the purpose?" asked Guan Yin Zi. "Yes!" said Lie Zi. "Good!" said Guan Yin Zi; "keep it clearly in your memory; see that you don't forget it. The rule for any progress is that before undertaking anything one should know why. The sage does not calculate whether he will succeed or come unstuck, and the chances for and against. He fixes his aim, and then moves towards it." (Lie Zi, chapter 8).

Archery; artificial and natural.

Lie Zi was practising archery in the presence of Bo Hun Wu Ren, with a cup of water attached to his left elbow. He drew the bow to its maximum with his right hand, let fly, fitted another arrow, let fly again, and so on, without upsetting the water in the cup. Bo Hun Wu Ren said to him: "Your archery is that of an archer wholly occupied with his aim (artificial archery), not that of an archer indifferent to his aim (natural archery). Come up some high mountain with me, to the edge of a precipice, and let's see if you can still keep this presence of mind!" The two men did so. Bo Hun Wu Ren crouched at the edge of the precipice, his back to the chasm, his heels sticking out into space. (Note that the archer must move backwards to tension the bow). Then he greeted Lie Zi according to the rites, before starting to shoot. But Lie Zi, seized with vertigo, was already lying on the ground, the sweat running down to his heels. Bo Hun Wu Ren said to him: "The superior man plunges his gaze into the depths of the earth, the heights of the sky, the far distant horizon, without his mind being moved. It seems to me that your eyes are haggard, and that if you were to shoot you would miss your aim." (Lie Zi, chapter 2).

Archery; the secret of mental continuity.

When Gan Ying, the famous archer, drew his bow, birds and beasts delivered themselves to him, without waiting for the arrow. His disciple Fei Wei surpassed him. Fei Wei took Ji Chang as his disciple. He began by saying to him: "First learn not to blink and then I will teach you archery." Ji Chang taught himself in the following way: When his wife was weaving, he lay on his back under the loom, fixing his eyes on the criss-cross threads and the shuttle which passed to and fro. After two years of this exercise, his eyes became so fixed that a point could touch them without making him blink. Then Ji Chang went to find Fei Wei, and told him he was ready. "Not yet," said Fei Wei; "you still need to learn to fix on a point. When you can see it enlarged (through the power of your intention) to the point where it could not be missed, then come back, and I will teach you archery." Ji Chang hung up by his window a long yak-hair on which clung a flea. He then exercised himself by fixing his sight on the flea when the sun passed behind it and shone straight in his eyes. (Note: this should not be taken literally for such a practice could result in blindness. Also fleas do not have a centralised heart, - ed.) Day after day the flea appeared bigger. After three year's practice it looked enormous, and he could distinguish its heart. When he became able to pierce the flea's heart without his arrow breaking the hair, he went to find Fei Wei. "Now!" said the latter, "you have learnt archery; there is nothing else I can teach you." However Ji Chang told himself he had no other rival in the world but his master, and he resolved to do away with him (in one of those contests of skill that archers held in those times). The two men met on a plain, took up their positions, and shot against each other simultaneously. At each shot the arrows struck each other at the half-way point, and fell dead without raising any dust. But Ji Chang had put an extra arrow in his quiver, which he shot last, intending to pierce his unarmed master. Fei Wei parried the arrow with a spiny branch (which he had just time to pick up, for he had not expected treachery). Then, having put down their bows, the two men saluted each other on the ground, weeping with emotion and promising to be like father and son to each other. They also vowed to each other with a blood bond not to tell anyone the secret of their art (of mental continuity). (Lie Zi, chapter 5).

Concentration on one: the fighting cock.

Ji Xing Zi was training a fighting cock for Emperor Xuan of the Zhou Dynasty. After ten days, when asked for news, he said: "It is not ready to fight; it is still vain and headstrong." Ten days later, he said: "Not yet, it is still nervous and passionate." After another ten days, he said: "Now it is ready; it no longer pays attention to the sounds made by other members of its species; it is moved by their sight no more than if it were made of wood. No other cock will be able to hold out against it." (Zhuang Zi, ch. 19).

Different uses; the cream:

A family of silkworm keepers from Song possessed the recipe for a cream which prevented the hands of those who separated the cocoons from chapping or cracking. They sold their recipe to a foreigner for a hundred pieces of gold, and considered they had made a good profit. Now the foreigner came to be admiral of the fleet for the King of Wu, and he commanded a naval expedition against Yue. It was winter. Having used his cream to protect the hands of his sailors from chilblains, he won a great victory which procured for him a vast fief; so two uses of the same cream produced a small sum, and an immense fortune. (Zhuang Zi, ch. 1).

Same action; different times.

A certain Shi of Lu had two sons, one wise, and the other brave. The wise one went and offered himself to the Marquis of Qi, who accepted him and nominated him tutor to his children. The brave one went and offered himself to the King of Chu, who was pleased with him and made him a wealthy and noble general. Now a neighbour of Shi, called Meng, also had two sons, one wise and the other brave. As he was very poor, the luck of the Shi family filled him with envy and he asked them how they had gone about it. They told him quite simply. The wise Meng went straight away and offered himself to the King of Qin. The latter said: "In these war-like times I need only soldiers; this scholar who teaches goodness and fairness will harm my kingdom." And he ordered him to be castrated and sent back home. The brave Meng offered himself to the Marquis of Wei. The latter said: "My state is small and weak and I must be careful not to annoy my great and formidable neighbours. I must stay peaceful. Any sign of warlike intentions could cost me my Marquisate. I cannot employ this able man without taking a grave risk. On the other hand, if I send him away without making him a cripple, he will go and offer himself to another prince and ruin me." Therefore he ordered that he should be sent back home with one of his feet cut off. When old Meng saw his two sons return mutilated, he beat his chest with sadness, and went to reproach father Shi. The latter said to him: "At fortunate times, one succeeds; at unfortunate times, only bad things happen. Your sons and mine took exactly the same steps. The results have been absolutely different. This has to do uniquely with destiny, and not at all with the methods used. Fortune and misfortune are not ruled by mathematical laws. What succeeded yesterday may go wrong today. What went wrong today will perhaps go well tomorrow. Success comes from acting at the right moment, but there are no rules that allow one to determine that moment. The wisest are sometimes wrong about it, even Kong Qiu and Lü Shang have known failures." When the Meng family had heard these explanations they were satisfied, and said: "Thank you; don't say any more; we have understood." (Lie Zi, ch. 8).

Steal from nature, steal from others.

In the land of Qi a certain Guo was very rich. In the land of Song a certain Xiang was very poor. The poor man went to ask the rich man how he had gained his wealth. "By stealing!" said the latter. "At the end of the first year I had the necessary, after two years I had plenty, and at the end of the third year I had become opulent and a person of great distinction." Misunderstanding the word 'stealing,' Xiang questioned him no further. Full of joy, he took a holiday and soon set himself to work, climbing walls or breaking through them, laying his hands on anything that suited him. He was soon arrested and had to repay everything. He lost even the little he had before, but was happy to have got off so lightly. In the belief that he had been misled, he went and made bitter reproaches to Guo. "How did you go about it?" asked Guo, quite astonished. When Xiang had told him his methods, Guo said: "Ah, it was not by that kind of theft that I became rich. I stole my wealth from heaven and earth, from the rain, the mountains and the plains, according to the times and circumstances. I appropriated the fruits of nature, wild animals of the plains and fish and turtles from the water. Everything I possess I have stolen from nature, but before it belonged to anyone; whereas you have stolen what heaven had already given to other men." Xiang went away discontented, thinking Guo had misled him again. He met the Master of the Eastern Suburb and explained his case to him. "But of course," said the latter, "every appropriation is a theft. Even a living being is a theft of a portion of the harmony of the yin and the yang; and every appropriation of a material being is a theft from nature. But one must distinguish theft from theft. Stealing from nature is a common theft committed by everyone, and it is not subject to punishment. Stealing from others is the theft which is subject to punishment. All men live by stealing from heaven and earth, without however being thieves." (Lie Zi, chapter 1).

Sacrificial cattle.

A prince sent an invitation to Zhuang Zi to become his minister, and the latter replied to the envoy: 'The ox destined for sacrifice is dressed in an embroidered cloth and receives choice food. But one day they take it to the great temple to be slaughtered; at that moment it would have preferred to have been the commonest ox of all, on the worst pasture of all; it is the same for the ministers of princes; honours first, disgrace and death in its time.' (Zhuang Zi, chapter 32,)

Universal folly.

A certain Pang of the Principality of Qin had a son. When quite small this child seemed intelligent, but when he grew up his mentality seemed very strange. Singing made him cry, and he thought that white was black; perfumes were stinking; sugar was bitter, and good was bad. In a nutshell, in thoughts and things, in each and everything, he was the opposite of other people. A certain Yang said to his father: "This is quite an extra-ordinary case; you should go to Lu, where the scholars are very wise, and ask for some advice." The father of the topsy-turvy child set off in the direction of Lu. When he was passing through Chen he met Lao Dan and told him about his son. Lao Dan replied: "Is that why you think he is crazy? All men of these times are mad. They all take evil for good, and make rules of conduct to serve their personal gain. There is no one who does not suffer from it. One fool per family, a family of fools per village, a village of fools per principality, a principality of fools in the empire; that would be tolerable, strictly speaking. But now the whole empire is crazy with the same folly as your son's; if not, it is you who are crazy for thinking differently from the others. Who will ever define the rules of feelings, sounds, colours, scent, tastes, of good and evil? I am not certain if I myself am wise, but I am certain that the scholars of Lu (who claim to define these things) are the worst inseminators of folly. And you are going to ask them to cure your son for you? Believe me, save yourself the expense of a useless journey and take the shortest route back home." Lie Zi, ch. 3).

Imagination and suggestion.

A child born in the Principality of Yen (in the far north) had been taken to the Kingdom of Chu (in the far south of the empire) where he was brought up and spent all his life. As an old man he returned to the land of his birth. Half-way there, as he approached the principal town of Jin, his travelling companions tried to make fun of him by saying: "Here is the principal town of Yen, your country." Our man, believing them, became pale and sad. Then, showing him a mound of the Earth Spirit, they said: "This is the mound of your native village." The man sighed sadly. Then they showed him a house and said: "Here is the home of your ancestors." The man burst into tears. Finally, showing him some tombs, they said: "And here are their tombs." With these words our man burst into lamentation. Then his companions uncovered their hoax. "We have fooled you," they said. "This is Jin, it's not Yen." Our man was very confused, but from then on he controlled his feelings so well that, when he reached Yen and truly saw its principal town, his village mound, the home of his ancestors and their tombs, he showed little or no emotion. (Lie Zi, chapter 3).

The three doctors.

Ji Liang, a friend of Yang Zhu, had fallen ill, and after seven days was near the end. Shedding tears, his son ran to all the surrounding doctors. The invalid said to Yang Zhu: "Try to get some sense into my imbecile of a son." Yang Zhu therefore recited to the son the verse: "What heaven does not know (the future), how can man guess it? It is not true that heaven blesses, or curses, anyone. We know you and I that fate is blind and inescapable. What can doctors and magicians do about that?" But the son did not desist, and brought three doctors, a Jiao, a Yu, and a Lu. All three examined the patient, one after the other. The Jiao said: "In your case heat and cold are in disequilibrium, empty and full are out of proportion; you have eaten, played, thought, and tired yourself too much; your illness is natural, and not the effect of some evil influx; although serious, it can be cured." "This one recites the claptrap of the books; send him away without more ado," said Ji Liang. The Yu said to the patient: "In your case, you came from your mother's womb with a defective vitality, and afterwards took in more milk than you could digest. The origin of your illness goes back to that time. As it is inveterate it can hardly be completely cured." "This one speaks well," said Ji Liang; "we should invite him to dinner." The Lu said to the patient: "Not heaven, nor man, nor a spectre, are the cause of your illness. Born with a composite body, you are subject to the law of dissolution, and must understand that the time approaches; no medicine will do anything for you." "This one has spirit," said Ji Liang; "we should pay him generously." Ji Liang took no medicine, and was completely cured (destiny). Caring for life does not lengthen it; lack of care does not shorten it. A high regard for the body does not improve it, contempt for it does not cause it to deteriorate. In this matter the consequences do not correspond with the actions. Often they seem even diametrically opposite, without being so in reality, for fate has no opposite. One lives or one dies, because one should live or die. Neither care nor negligence of life nor the body do anything; neither one way nor the other. That is why You Xiong said to King Wen: "Man can neither add to nor take away from his stature; all his calculations can do nothing about that." In the same vein, Lao Dan said to Guan Yin Zi: "When heaven does not wish something, who can say why?" In other words, it is better to keep oneself in peace, than to try to know the intentions of heaven, to predict what is good-omened and ill-omened. (They are vain calculations, all being ruled by unpredictable, inescapable, destiny). Lie Zi, chapter 6).

The scrupulous one.

In the east, a certain Yuan Xing Mu who was travelling collapsed on the road. Robber Qiu of Hu Fu, who was passing, put some food in his mouth. After the third mouthful, Yuan Xing Mu came round. "Who are you?" he asked. "I am Qiu from Hu Fu," said the other. "Oh!" said Yuan Xing Mu; "aren't you a robber? And you have made me eat your food? I am an honest man; I will not keep it." And, resting on both hands, our man tried to make himself vomit with such violent efforts that he expired there and then. He acted stupidly. If Qiu of Hu Fu was a robber, his food had nothing to do with robbing. In applying to the food what should be applied to the robber, this Yuan Xing Mu showed that he was lacking in logic. (Lie Zi, ch. 8).

Recipe against death.

Once, someone claimed to have the recipe for avoiding death. The Prince of Yen sent a deputy to ask him for it. When the deputy arrived, the man with the recipe had died. The prince blamed the deputy for having gone there too late, and was going to punish him. One of his favourites said to him: "If this man truly had the recipe for not dying, he would certainly not have deprived himself of its benefit. Now he is dead. Therefore he did not have the formula. It could not, therefore, have procured immortality for you." The prince gave up the idea of punishing the deputy. A certain Qi who also had a great desire to avoid death, was also grieved by the death of this man. A certain Fu mocked him, saying that, since the man was dead, it was unreasonable to regret the loss of his ineffective secret. A certain Hu said that Fu had spoken badly for it can happen that he who has a secret does not know how to make use of it; just as some others happen to produce a result (by chance or experiment), without having the formula. A man of Wei was good at incantations. When he was near to death, he taught his son his formulae. The latter recited the formulae perfectly, but with no effect. He taught them to another, who could recite them with the same effect the father had. "Since a living soul was able to act effectively with the formulae of a dead soul, I ask myself (says Lie Zi) if the dead would also be able to act effectively with the formulae of the living?" (Life and death; two forms of the same being). (Lie Zi, ch. 8).

Autosuggestion.

In the Principality of Qi a poor man was always begging in the market-place of the town. Tired by his entreaties, the people stopped giving him anything. Then the poor man went into the service of a veterinary of the princely family Tian and earned enough to avoid dying of starvation. They said to him that to serve a veterinary was a disgrace. He replied: "To be reduced to begging passes as the worst disgrace. Now, I was a beggar. How can serving a veterinary be a disgrace for me? It is a step up the ladder." — A man of Song found half of a divided contract on the road, which someone had lost. He folded it painstakingly, carefully noting the way it had been cut, and confided to his neighbour that he was about to come into a fortune. He was wrong in thinking that the way in which he had obtained the first half must also give him the second half. — A man had a dead tree in his garden. His neighbour said to him: "A dead tree is an ill-omened object." The man cut the tree down. The neighbour then asked him to let him have the wood. The man then suspected that the neighbour had made him cut down the tree with that in mind, and took offence. He was wrong. The request that followed does not prove that there was a previous intention. — A man had lost his axe, and suspected that his neighbour's son had stolen it. The more he thought about it, the more he believed it. Therefore, to him, the manner, expression, speech, in fact everything about this boy seemed to make him a thief. When he cleared out his manure pit, he found his axe. The next day, when he saw his neighbour's son, he saw him as the most honest boy that ever was. — When Bai Gong was plotting to avenge his father's death he slipped and fell, and the spike of the handle of his horsewhip pierced his chin without him feeling anything. The people of Zheng who knew about this, said: 'If he could not feel that, what would he feel?" He must have been so absorbed in plotting his revenge, that he did not notice his fall, or the wound. — A man of Qi was suddenly taken by so great a desire for gold, that he got up in the morning, dressed, went straight to the money-changer's stall in the market, grabbed a gold piece and walked away. The guards caught him and said to him: "What made you steal in a place so full of people?" "I only saw the gold," he said; "I did not see the people." (Lie Zi, ch. 8).

Twilight and shadow.

Twilight (symbolising the half-wise) said to Shadow (Daoist ignorance): 'You are up and down, brought together and then scattered, seated then standing, moving and then resting; what is the reason for all this?' 'I don't know,' said Shadow. 'I am like that, without knowing why. I am like the cast off skin of the cicada or the snake, an accessory, a thing having no existence of its own. I am even less real than that. With the light of day, or the fire, I appear; I disappear when the light fades. I depend for my being, on an object, which depends on the universal being, for its being. When it appears, I appear also; when it disappears, I disappear also; when it dies, I die also with it. I cannot give you an explanation of my movements.' Thus everything is passive, existing through the Principle, depending on the Principle. Knowing this, the disciple of wisdom should above all be profoundly humble. (Zhuang Zi, ch. 27).

Chaos operated on.

Carried Away, King of the Southern Sea, and Turned Away, King of the Northern Sea, were on good terms with Chaos, King of the Centre. They asked themselves what service they could render him. "Men have seven orifices" (two eyes, ears, nostrils, and a mouth) they said. This poor Chaos hasn't any. Let's make some for him." Setting themselves to work, they made him one orifice a day. On the seventh day Chaos died (ceased to be Chaos). All beings should be left in their natural deprived state; one should not seek to perfect them artificially, otherwise they cease to be what they were and should remain. (Zhuang Zi, ch. 7).

The black pearl.

The Yellow Emperor had advanced as far as the north of the Red River, and climbed Mount Kun Lun in order to view the regions of the south, when he lost his black pearl (his treasure, his notion of the Principle, lost through having surrendered himself to his ambitious dreams). He made Science look for it, but he could not recover it. Investigation and Discussion could not find it either. Finally, Abstraction recovered it. The Yellow Emperor said to himself: "Is it not strange that it was found by Abstraction, considered by the common people to be the least practical of faculties." (Zhuang Zi, ch. 12).

The crushed pearl.

A politician in quest of a master to serve had paid court to the King of Song, and received ten cart-loads of presents which he showed to Zhuang Zi with a puerile ostentation. Zhuang Zi said to him: 'A poor family lived by the river, laboriously weaving mats (a poorly paid craft). The son of the family dived under the water and brought up a pearl worth a good thousand pieces of gold. As soon as the father saw it, he said: "Take a stone and break it, quickly. Pearls of this size are only found at the bottom of an abyss, under a black dragon's chin. No doubt the dragon was sleeping when you took it. When he awakes, he will look for it, and should he find it here, it would be to our loss." Now the Kingdom of Song is also an abyss, and its king is worse than the black dragon. No doubt he was distracted when you put your hands on these ten cart-loads of good things. If he should change his mind, you will be crushed under his foot.' (Zhuang Zi, chapter 32).

The Yellow Emperor's symphony.

Biemen Cheng said to the Yellow Emperor: "When I listened to the performance of your Xian Chi symphony near Lake Dong Ting, the first part made me afraid, the second made me dizzy, the third gave me a sensation of vagueness from which I have still not recovered." "That is as it should be," said the emperor. "That symphony contains everything. It is a human expression of heavenly action, of universal evolution. The first part expresses the contrast of terrestrial facts which come under heavenly influence; the struggle of the five elements, the succession of the four seasons; birth and decay of plant life; action and reaction of heavy and light, light and darkness, sound and silence; the renewal of animal life in springtime, to the sound of thunder, after the winter torpor; the institution of human laws, civil and military offices, etcetera; all abruptly, with neither introductions nor transitions; in shocking sounds, a suite of dissonances, like the chain of births and deaths, of the appearance and disappearance of ephemeral earthly things. It should have made you afraid. The second part of the symphony renders, in soft or loud, prolonged and drawn out sounds, the continuity of the action of the yin and the yang, of the course of the two great luminaries, of the arrival of the living and the departure of the dead. It is this suite, continuing until it faded away, that made you dizzy by its infinitude, to the point that, no longer knowing where you were, you clung to a tree trunk, gasping with vertigo and anxiety caused by the void. The third part of the symphony expresses the productions of nature, the unfolding of destinies. Hence the effervescence followed by calm; the murmur of the great forests, then a mysterious silence. For that is how beings are born, coming, in streams and waves, from an unknown origin, and leaving for an unknown destination. The sage alone can understand this harmony, for he alone understands nature and destiny. Heavenly joy, which is felt but cannot be explained, consists in grasping the threads of becoming, before being, whilst they are still held by the craft of cosmic weaving. It consists, as Master Yen has sung, in hearing that which has not yet any sound, seeing that which has not yet any form, which fills heaven and earth, and embraces space, the Principle, the motor of cosmic evolution. Not knowing that, you remained vague. My explanations have made you pass from this vagueness to the knowledge of the Principle. Guard this well." (Zhuang Zi, ch. 14).

The pleasure of fish.

Zhuang Zi and Hui Zi were taking their recreation on a footbridge over a stream; Zhuang Zi said: 'Look how the fish are jumping; that is how they take their pleasure.' 'You are not a fish,' said Hui Zi; 'how do you know what their pleasure is?' 'You are not I,' said Zhuang Zi; 'how do you know that I don't know they take pleasure in that?' 'I am not you,' said Hui Zi, 'and in consequence I don't know what you know or don't know, that I agree; but in any case I know that you are not a fish, and it remains established therefore that you don't know what is their pleasure.' 'You are taken,' said Zhuang Zi. 'Let's come back to your first question. You asked me "how do you know what their pleasure is?" By that phrase you have admitted that I know it; because you would not have asked me the "how" of what you knew I did not know. And now, how did I know it; by direct observation from the footbridge of the stream, a means unknown to the sophists of that time, quibblers who do not observe. (Zhuang Zi, ch. 17).

The sea-bird.

.....Opportunism alone makes for success. Everything does not suit everyone. One should not judge others after oneself. Once, a sea bird fell down at the gates of the capital of Lu. As it was an extraordinary phenomenon, the marquis thought perhaps it was a transcendent being visiting his principality. He went therefore in person to care for the bird, and carried it to the temple of his ancestors, where he gave it a feast. They performed the Giu Shao symphony of Emperor Shun in front of it. They offered it a great sacrifice, a bull, a billy-goat, and a pig. However the bird, its eyes haggard and looking heart-broken, did not touch the stew nor taste the wine. After three days it died of hunger and thirst. This was because the marquis, judging the tastes of the bird after his own, had treated it as he treated himself, and not as one should treat a bird. A sea bird needs space, forests and plains, rivers and lakes, fish for its food, freedom to fly and rest where it wills. Hearing the speech of men was a punishment for this poor bird; how much more the music they played for it, and all the movement they made around it. If one were to play the Giu Shao symphony of Shun, or likewise the Man Chi symphony of the Yellow Emperor, on the banks of Lake Dong Ting, the birds would fly away, quadrupeds would hide themselves, fish would dive into the deepest waters, and men, on the contrary, would listen and marvel. Fish live in the water, and men die in it. The nature of beings is diverse, and their tastes are not the same. It is the same for men, there are differences; what pleases some does not please others. Thus the ancient sages did not assume that all men had the same capacity, and they did not employ no matter whom for no matter what. They classed men according to their works, and dealt with them according to their results. This adequate and just recognition of individuals is a condition for any success….(Zhuang Zi, ch. 18).

Monkey Island.

Whilst the King of Wu was boating on the Blue River, he landed on Monkey Island. The monkeys saw him coming, and fled and hid themselves in the brushwood. One alone stayed behind, playing about as if to flout him. The king shot an arrow at it. The monkey snatched it in flight. Nettled, the king ordered all of his followers to give chase to the impertinent monkey, which soon succumbed to the number of assailants. In front of its corpse, the king gave the following lesson to Yen Bu Yi, his favourite: 'This monkey perished because it provoked me by its ostentation and know-how. Watch yourself! Don't imitate it. Do not lose my favour through your bravado.' Scared, Yen Bu Yi asked Dong Wu to teach him simplicity. At the end of three years everyone spoke well of him (and he improved all the time). (Zhuang Zi, chapter 24).

The skull.

When Lie Zi, who was travelling in the Principality of Wei, stopped to eat his food by the wayside, one of his companions picked up an old skull and showed it to him. Lie Zi looked at it and said to his disciple Bai Feng. "He and I know that the difference between life and death is only imaginary, he through experience, and I through reasoning. He and I know that to cling to life and to fear death is unreasonable, life and death being only successive phases. Everything passes according to time or circumstance, through successive states, without changing essentially. (Lie Zi, ch. 1)

The Shang Rapid.

Yen Yuan, the favourite disciple, said to Confucius: 'When I was crossing the Shang rapids, the ferryman handled his craft with a marvellous dexterity. I said to him: "How can one learn to manoeuvre so well?" "A swimmer," he said, "learns it easily; a diver knows it without having to learn". I did not understand him. Can you explain it to me?' 'Yes,' said Confucius (speaking as a Daoist master): 'A swimmer thinks little of the water, being familiar with its dangers, which he scarcely fears any more; a diver does not think of it at all, being in his element in water. The feeling of danger affects the swimmer a little; he has almost complete use of his natural faculties. The feeling of danger does not affect the diver at all; he is one with the ferry-boat and in consequence governs it perfectly. In an archery contest, if the prize is an earthenware object of little value, the archer will be uninfluenced and have free use of all his skill; if the prize is a belt buckle in bronze or jade, the archer will be influenced, and his aim less certain. If the proposed prize is a golden object, his aim will be strongly influenced and quite uncertain. The same man, the same talent, but more, or less, influenced by an exterior object. All distractions cause foolishness and nervousness.' (Zhuang Zi, ch. 19).

The Lu Liang Falls.

One day when Confucius was admiring the Lu Liang Cascade, a fall of two hundred and forty feet which produces a boiling torrent over a great distance, so rapid that neither cayman nor fish can swim against it, he perceived a man swimming amongst the swirling waters. Thinking he was in despair and seeking death, he told his disciples to follow along the bank in order to pull him out should he pass within reach. Now, several hundred paces further down, this man came out of the water himself, undid his hair in order to dry it, and went along the bank at the foot of the cliff, humming. Confucius reached him and said: "When I saw you swimming in the torrent, I thought you wished to end your life. Then, seeing the ease with which you came out of the water, I took you for a transcendent being. But no, you are a man, of flesh and blood. Please tell me how one can sport oneself like that in the water." "I don't know the how of it," said the man. "When I began, I applied myself to the task; later it became easy for me, and at last I could do it naturally, unconsciously. I allow myself to be drawn in by the centre of the whirlpool, then to be thrown up by the peripheral swirl. I follow the movement of the water, without making any movement myself. That is all I can say about it." (Lie Zi, ch. 2)

Destiny; the cow.

A man of Song practised humanity and justice. His family had done so for three generations. One day, without one being able to find out the cause, his black cow gave birth to an entirely white calf. The man sent to

Confucius to ask what this phenomenon portended. "It is a good omen," said Confucius; "this calf should he sacrificed to the Sovereign on High." A year later, without any known cause, the father of the family became blind. Soon after, his black cow gave birth to a second white calf. The father sent his son again to ask Confucius what this portended. The son said: "After the last consultation you lost your sight; what's the good of asking again?" "Go!" said the father. "The words of the sages sometimes appear wrong but they prove right given time. Let us assume that the time has not yet come, so go!" The son went and asked Confucius, who said again: "It is a good omen. Offer it to the Sovereign on High." The son reported the reply to his father, who ordered him to carry it out. A year later the son also became blind. Now suddenly the Chus invaded Song and laid siege to its capital. The famine became so bad that families exchanged their children for food. All able-bodied men had to defend the ramparts. More than half of them perished. In this disaster, since the two blind ones were unable to be of any service, they were exempted from duty. When the siege was raised they suddenly recovered their sight. Destiny had made them blind for their own safety. (Lie Zi, ch. 8).

Misguided piety.

Tian of Qi made offerings to his ancestors, and gave a great banquet to a thousand guests, each of whom brought the customary present. One of the guests brought fish and wild geese. On seeing them Tian sighed piously and said: "Look how well heaven treats men; it not only makes diverse cereals grow; it also causes the birth of fish and birds for the use of men." All the guests agreed in a servile chorus. Alone the son of the Bao family, a boy of twelve, came forward and said: "what you have just said is not quite right. Even heaven and earth are beings like all beings. There are no superior beings, there are no inferior ones. It is a fact that the stronger and more ingenious eat the weaker and less clever ones, but one should not conclude that the latter were made for the use of the former. Man eats the beings he can eat, but heaven did not cause the birth of these beings in order that man should eat them. Otherwise one would have to say that heaven has caused men to be born in order that mosquitoes could bite them, and tigers and wolves devour them." (Lie Zi, chapter 8)

Personal sacrifice.

Zhu Li Shu served Duke Ao of Ju. Finding that he was treated too coldly, he left, and went to live as a hermit at the seaside, eating mackerel in summer, and acorns and chestnuts in winter. When Duke Ao died, Zhu Li Shu said farewell to his friends, and declared that he would commit suicide. His friends said to him: "You left the duke because he treated you coldly, and now you want to kill yourself because he is dead; you are lacking in logic." "Not at all!" said Zhu Li Shu. "I left the duke because he showed me too little favour. I am going to kill myself because, now, he can never show me favour. I want to teach the masters of the future to treat their officials properly, and leave officials the example of a more than usual devotion." This Zhu Li Shu sacrificed his life for a high ideal. (Lie Zi, ch. 8).

Three sacrifices.

Shun offered his empire to his old friend Wu Ze. 'For shame,' said the latter. 'You left the country for the court, and now you wish that I also should degrade myself. I no longer know you.' That said, Wu Ze went and threw himself into the Qing Ling Chasm. Before attacking Jie (the tyrant), Tang (the future emperor) consulted Bian Sui, who replied: 'That is none of my business.' 'Then whom should I consult?' asked Tang. 'I don't know,' said Bian Sui. Tang addressed himself to Wu Guang, who also replied: 'It is none of my business, I don't know.' Then Tang said: 'If I were to ask Yi Yin?' 'Perfect!' said Wu Guang. 'Coarse and dull, this man has what it needs to serve your designs; moreover that's all that he has.' Advised by Yi Yin, Tang attacked Jie, vanquished him, and then offered the throne to Bian Sui. The latter said: 'My refusal to advise you should have made you understand that I wish to have nothing to do with a thief; and here you are offering me your loot! Must this century be so perverse that a man without conscience should twice try to dirty me by his contact! No one will do me such an injury a third time.' That said, Bian Sui drowned himself in the River Chou. Then Tang offered the throne to Wu Guang with this patter: 'A sage (Yi Yin) made the plan (of Jie's dethronement); a brave (Tang) executed it; now the good (Wu Guang) should mount the throne, conforming to the traditions of the ancients.' Wu Guang refused in these terms: 'Dethroning an emperor is to lack etiquette; killing his subjects, is to lack goodness; profiting from another's crimes would be to lack decency. I hold myself to the traditional maxims which forbid accepting any post from an iniquitous master, and treading on the ground of an empire without principles. I refuse to be honoured by you, and wish to see you no more.' That said, Wu Guang tied a large stone on his back, and threw himself into the River Lu. (Zhuang Zi, chapter 28).

Robbers: different action same result.

Niu Que was a famous scholar of Shang Di. Whilst he was going down to Han Dan, in open country, he was assailed by robbers who took everything, even his clothes, without his trying to stop them. He then went off without showing any sign of sadness. Astonished, a robber ran after him, and asked him why he was not distressed. "Because the sage prefers life to possessions," he said. "Ah!" said the robber, "you are a sage." When he told the others, they said: "If he is a sage, he must be going to see the Prince of Zhao. He is going to accuse us, and we will be lost. Let's kill him first, whilst there is still time." They ran after Niu Que and killed him. Now a man of Yen who heard this story, assembled his family and said: "If you ever meet robbers, don't do what Niu Que of Shang Di did." Sometime later, the younger brother of this man was going to Qin when he met some robbers near the pass. Remembering the advice of his older brother, he put up all possible resistance. When the thieves left, he ran after them, demanding back what they had taken, and hurling insults. This was too much. "We left you your life, against the usual custom," they said to him. "But since, by following us, you expose us to the risk of being captured, we shall have to kill you." Four or five who accompanied him, were killed with him. (Do not boast; efface yourself) (Lie Zi, chapter 8).

3. DAO, THE PRINCIPLE (THE WAY).

Dao is ineffable, unnameable, unchangeable:

The Principle that can be enunciated is not the one that always was. The being that can be named is not the one that was at all times. Before time, there was an ineffable, unnameable being.

When it was still unnameable, it conceived heaven and earth. When it had thus become nameable, it gave birth to the multitude of beings.

These two acts are but one, under two different denominations; the unique act of generation; that is the mystery of the beginning, the mystery of mysteries; the door through which have issued, on to the scene of the universe, all the marvels which it contains.

The knowledge that one has of the universal Principle depends on one's state of mind; the mind habitually free from passion knows its mysterious essence; the habitually passionate mind knows only its effects. (Lao Zi, chapter 1).

(The traditional commentaries on the above chapter may be summarized as follows: Before time, and throughout time, there has been a self-existing being, eternal, infinite, complete and omnipresent. This 'being' cannot be named or spoken about, because human terms only apply to perceptible beings. Now the primordial being was primitively, and still is essentially, non-sentient, non-perceptible. Outside this being, before the beginning, there was nothing. It is referred to as *wu*, without form, *huan*, mystery, or Dao, the Principle. The period when there was not as yet any sentient being, when the essence alone of the Principle existed, is called *xian tian*, before heaven. This essence possessed two immanent properties, the *yin* concentration, and the *yang*, expansion, which were exteriorized one 'day' under the perceptible forms of heaven (yang) and earth (yin). That 'day' marked the beginning of time. From that day Dao, the Principle, can be named by the double term of heaven and earth. The heaven-earth binomial emits all sentient beings. The heaven-earth binomial is called *you*, sentient being, which through *de*, the virtue of the Principle, generates all of its products that fill up the world. The period since heaven and earth were exteriorized is called *hou tian,* after heaven. The state yin of concentration and rest, of imperceptibility, which was that of the Principle before time, is its inherent sate. The state yang of expansion and action, of manifestation in sentient beings, is its state in time, in some ways inappropriate. To these two states of Dao (the Principle) there corresponds, in the faculty of human awareness, rest and activity, or, put another way, empty and full. When the human mind produces ideas, is full of images, is moved by passion, then it is only able to know the effects of the Principle, distinct perceptible things. When the human mind, absolutely arrested, is completely empty and calm, it is a pure and clear mirror, capable of reflecting the ineffable and unnameable essence of the Principle itself. The following passages restate in new language and expand the above:)

This is all that we can understand of the Principle and of its action as producer. Seeking to detail it further using words and numbers would be a waste of time. Let us hold ourselves to this grand idea. (Lao Zi, Chapter 5)

Looking one does not see it, for it is invisible. Listening, one does not hear it, for it is silent. Touching, one does not feel it, for it is impalpable. These three attributes must not be separated, for they designate one and the same being. (Lao Zi, chapter 14).

The Principle is indistinct and indeterminate, mysterious and obscure. In its indistinctness and indetermination there are types, a multitude of beings. In its mystery and obscurity there is an essence which is reality. (Lao Zi chapter 21).

There is a being, of unknown origin, which existed before heaven and earth; imperceptible and undefined, unique and immutable, omnipresent, the mother of everything there is.

I do not know it by its own name. I designate it by the word Dao, the Principle. If it were necessary to name it, one would call it the Great, great going forth, great distance and great return; (the principle of the great cyclical evolution of the cosmos, of the becoming and ending of all beings).

The name Great befits (proportionately) four (superimposed) beings; the emperor, earth, heaven (the classical triad), and Dao the Principle. The emperor owes his greatness to the earth (his theatre,) earth owes its greatness to heaven (of which it is the fruit). Heaven owes its greatness to the Principle (of which it is the principle agent; a borrowed greatness, as one can see whereas) the Principle owes its essential greatness to its non-derived, uncreated existence. (Lao Zi, chapter 25).

The Principle has no name of its own. It is nature. This nature so unapparent is stronger than anything. If princes and emperors were to conform themselves to it, all beings would collaborate with them spontaneously; heaven and earth would act in perfect harmony, sprinkling a sweet dew (the best possible omen); the people would be governable without the need for constraint. (Lao Zi, chapter 32).

Dao is the palladium of all beings. It is the treasure of the good (that by which they are good), and the salvation of the wicked (that which prevents them from perishing).

It is to it that one should be grateful for affectionate words, and the noble behaviour of good people. It is with regard to it, that the wicked should not be rejected.

It is for that reason (for the conservation and development of the part of Dao, the Principle that is in all beings) that the emperor and the great ministers were instituted. Not so that they should become complacent with their sceptre and their ancient four-horsed chariot; but in order that they should meditate on the Principle (thereby advancing themselves in knowledge, and in the development of others).

Why did the ancients make so much of the Principle? Is it not because it is the source of all good and the remedy for all evil? It is the noblest thing in the world. (Lao Zi, chapter 62).

What I (Lao Zi) teach is easy to understand and to practise, and yet the world neither understands nor practises it.

My precepts and procedures derive from a superior principle and procedure, the Principle and its virtue.

The world does not recognize the Principle which directs me, that is why it does not know me. Very few understand me. That makes my glory. It befalls me to be like the sage who is unrecognized from amongst the common people because of his humble appearance, even though his interior is filled with jewels. (Lao Zi, ch. 70)

In the writings of the Yellow Emperor it is said: "When a substance is projected, it does not produce a new substance, but a shadow; when a sound resonates, it does not produce a new sound, but an echo; when formlessness is dying, it does not produce a new formlessness, but the sentient being." Each substance will have an end. Heaven and earth are substances, and they will end just as I will; if one can call what is only a change of state, an end. For the Principle, from which everything originates, will not have an end, since it has no beginning, and is not subject to the laws of duration. Beings pass successively through the states of being living and non-living, of being material and non-material. The state of non-living is not produced by non-life, but follows on from the state of life (like its shadow, as mentioned above). The state of non-materiality is not produced by immateriality, but follows from the state of materiality (as its echo, referred to above). This successive alternation is surely inevitable. Each living thing will inevitably cease to live, and it will cease later on, inevitably, to be non-living, and will return of necessity to life. Therefore to wish to make one's life last and to escape death is to wish the impossible. — In the human composite, the vital spirit is the contribution of heaven and the body is the contribution of earth. Man begins by the aggregation of his vital spirit with the gross earthly elements, and ends by the union of the same spirit with the pure heavenly elements. When the vital spirit leaves the body, each of the two components returns to its origin. That is why we have a similar sounding word *(gui)* for 'dead' and for 'returned'. The dead are, in fact, returned to their own abode (the cosmos). The yellow Emperor has said: "the vital spirit returns through its door (in the Principle), the body returns to its origin (matter), and the individuality is done away with." (Lie Zi, chapter 1).

Now this Whole is the Principle, will, reality, non-acting, non-apparent; it can be transmitted but not grasped, apprehended but not seen. It has its essence and its root in itself. It existed, immutable, before heaven and earth were formed. It is the source of the transcendence of the heavenly beings and the Sovereign of the Annals and the Odes. It was, before formless matter, before space, before the world, before time; without one being able to call it high, profound, durable, ancient (since the absolute does not admit of relative epithets). Xi Wei knew it, and derived from this knowledge the astronomical laws. Fu Xi knew it, and took from this knowledge the physical laws. The bear (the pole-star) owes its imperturbable fixity to it. The sun and moon owe their regular courses to it. No one knows anything of its beginning or its end. (Zhuang Zi, chapter 6D)

At the centre of all things and superior to all, is the supreme Principle, unique and transforming itself into productive action. Heaven, the sky (physical instrument of the productive action of the Principle), is transcendent and acts without cease. The true sages also have the rule of letting heaven act without aiding it, letting the productive action act without interference, leaving the first Principle free. That is what is important in their eyes. For the rest, like the common practice, they are loving without affection, just without pretension, ritualistic without scrupulosity, active without fuss or ceremonies, legal without passion, devoted to the people and respectful of the rights of all. They do not consider any beings as particularly apt, and yet use them in the absence of better means. The ignorance of those who do not understand the action of heaven comes from the fact that they do not clearly understand the action of the supreme Principle, of which heaven is the instrument. Those who have no notion of the Principle are good-for-nothing, one should weep for them. There are two ways, the heavenly way and the human way. Concentrating oneself nobly on non-action is the way of heaven. Frittering oneself away, and troubling over details, is the human way. The two ways are very different. (Zhuang Zi, chapter 11).

A uniform transforming force emanates from the immense complex of heaven and earth; a unique law governs the mass of beings; a single ruler rules over a populous humanity. The ruler's power derives from the Principle; his person is chosen by heaven; so that he is referred to as mysterious, like the Principle. The rulers of antiquity abstained from all personal intervention, letting heaven govern through them. When the Principle acts through the ruler, his ministers and officials, then all beings respond by absolute submission to this just and enlightened government. Above the universe the first Principle influences heaven and earth, which transmit this influence to all beings, making for good government in the human world and bringing out talents and abilities. Looked at another way, all prosperity comes from the government, whose effectiveness derives from the Principle, through the intermediary of heaven and earth. That is why, when the ancient rulers desired nothing, there was an abundance in the world; they did not act, and everything evolved; they remained deep in meditation, and the people lived in the most perfect order. The old saying sums this up as follows: 'for one who is united with unity, everything prospers; to one who has no personal interest, even the subtle beings are subjected.'

How true are these words of the master; how great, how immense is the Principle which covers and supports all beings. The ruler should take great care to follow his inner sense. Natural action is heavenly action; the spontaneous verb is the heavenly influence; loving everyone and doing good to all beings is true goodness; fusing all differences into one is true greatness; not wishing to dominate others in any way is true breadth of spirit; possessing diverse things without dividing one's heart is true wealth; following the heavenly influence is the way to act; acting under this influence is to act effectively; serving as a docile intermediary of the Principle is perfection; not allowing one's determination to be affected by anything is constancy. The ruler should concentrate these six principles in himself, and then apply them to the government, and everything will follow its natural course. He should leave the gold in the rocks and the pearls in the depths, scorn wealth and honour and be indifferent to long life and early death. He should neither be vain in prosperity nor humiliated by adversity; he should disdain all the goods of this world, and he should not glorify himself because of his exaltation. His glory should be in understanding that all beings are a single universal complex, and that life and death are two modalities of the same being.

The Master has said: "the action of the Principle through heaven is infinite in its expansion, ungraspable in its subtlety. It resides, imperceptible, in all beings, as the cause of their being and their qualities. It is that which resonates in metals and sonorous flints. It is also in the blow that makes them resonate. Without it, nothing would be. The man who takes the qualities of a king from it, walks in simplicity and abstains from occupation with multiple things. Keeping himself with the origin, the source, united with unity, he knows like the genies by intuition in the Principle. In consequence his capacity extends to everything. When his spirit goes out through one of his senses, for example sight, as soon as it meets a being it grasps it, penetrates it and knows it in depth. This is because beings have become what they are through participation in the Principle and they are known through participation in the virtue of the Principle. Looking after beings, knowing their nature, acting on them with full knowledge of the Principle, these are the attributes of one born to be king. He appears unexpectedly on the scene of the world, plays his part and all beings give themselves to him. This is because he has received from the Principle the qualities which make a king. He sees in the darkness of the Principle, he hears the mute word of the Principle. For him, darkness is light, silence is harmony. He grasps being, at the most profound level of being; and his purpose, at the highest abstraction, is the Principle. Keeping himself at this height, entirely empty and denuded, he gives what is fitting to all. His action extends in time and space." (Zhuang Zi, chapter 12)

The influence of heaven acts freely, producing all beings. The Imperial influence, acting impartially, draws all the people to it. The sage's influence spreads uniformly, and everyone submits to him. Those who understand this mode of action of heaven, of the sage, and of the ideal head of state, concentrate themselves in meditative peace, which is the source of natural action. This peace is not an objective which the sage reaches by direct efforts. It consists in the negative fact that his heart is no longer moved by anything; it is acquired through abstraction. This is the principle of the sage's clear insight; just as perfectly calm water is clear and reflects even the hairs of the beard and eyebrows of one who looks in it. Nothing tends more towards rest, towards equilibrium, than water; so much so that the name of the perfect grade (level of water) is derived from it. Now just as rest clarifies water, it likewise clarifies the vital spirits, including the intelligence. The sage's heart, perfectly calm, is like a mirror which reflects heaven and earth, and all beings. Emptiness, peace, contentment, apathy, silence, comprehensive view, non-intervention; these make the formula of the influence of heaven and earth; of the Principle. The ancient emperors and sages knew this formula. Empty (of all passion) they kept the general laws truthfully. Peaceful (without any emotion) they acted effectively. Not intervening, leaving details to their officials, they were exempt from pleasure and pain, and in consequence they lived a long time. Is it not clear that emptiness, peace, contentment, apathy, silence, comprehensive view, non-intervention are the root of all good? He who understands this could be as good an emperor as Yao, and as good a minister as Shun. He could reign as king over the destiny of men; or as a sage, over their spiritual well-being. Whether he lives in retreat as an anchorite by the waters, in the mountains, or in the forests, or happens to be a world teacher, in each case he will be recognized and attract people to him. Yes, the speculations of the great sages, and the actions of the great kings, emanate from peace;

non-intervention makes them famous; abstraction elevates them above everything. Understand clearly the influence of heaven and earth, which is a kindly and tolerant non-intervention; it is the great root, the understanding with heaven. The principle of having such an understanding with men is practising an analogous non-intervention in government. Now human joy, supreme happiness, is living in harmony with men….

For the enlightened who possess this happiness there are no more complaints against heaven, no more resentment against men, no more worry about affairs, no more fear of ghosts. The action of the enlightened is confounded with the action of heaven, his rest with earth's repose. His closed spirit dominates the world; in death his inferior soul will not act badly (will dissipate itself peacefully), his superior soul will not wander as a ghost (will pass into another form). Yes! It is heavenly joy to follow the evolution of the Principle, in heaven, earth and all beings. This joy is the subsoil of the sage's heart. He draws his principle of government from this. (Zhuang Zi, chapter 13).

Lao Zi said: "Infinite in itself, the Principle penetrates the smallest of beings through its virtue. All are full of it. Immense in its extension, deeply profound, it embraces all and cannot be fathomed. All sentient beings and their qualities, all abstractions such as goodness and fairness, are ramifications of the Principle, but derived, far-off. The superior man understands this. Confucius, a common sage, is wrong on this point. Thus, when he governs, the superior man does not encumber himself with these details, and in consequence the government of the world only weighs lightly on him. He only occupies himself with the tiller, and avoids any contact with affairs. From above, his glance dominates everything. No particular interest touches him. He inquires only into the essence of things. He lets heaven and earth, and all beings, act, without the slightest mental fatigue, because he is without passion. Having penetrated as far as the Principle and identified his action with its action, he rejects artificial goodness and fairness, conventional rites and music; for his mind is dominated by a unique and fixed idea, not to intervene, to allow nature and time to act." (Zhuang Zi, chapter 13)

Dao has not been produced.

There is a producer that has not been produced, a transformer that is not transformed. This non-produced producer has produced the totality of beings, this non-transformed one transforms all beings. Since the beginning of production, the producer has not been able to stop producing; since the beginning of transformation, the transformer has not been able to stop transforming. The chain of productions and transformations is therefore uninterrupted, the producer and the transformer producing and transforming without cease. The yin-yang is the producer, (Dao, the Principle under its alternating double modality); the cycle of the four seasons is the transformer, (revolution of the heaven-earth binomial). The producer is immobile, the transformer comes and goes. The mobile and the immobile will last, always. (Lie Zi, chapter 1).

Lie Zi said: "Taken in isolation, heaven and earth have not every capacity, a sage has not every talent, a person has not every propriety. Heaven gives life and covers, earth supplies matter and supports, the sage teaches and amends, beings have each their own limited qualities. Heaven and earth have each their respective deficits which they compensate reciprocally; the sage has his defaults which oblige him to have recourse to others; all beings have to help each other. Heaven cannot supplant the earth, the earth cannot replace the sage, the sage cannot change the nature of beings, specific beings cannot leave their state. The action of heaven and earth consists in the alternation of the yin and the yang, the influence of the sage consists in the inculcation of goodness and fairness, the nature of beings is active or passive; all this is natural and immutable. Because there are products, there is a producer of these products. There is an author, of corporeal forms, of sounds, of colours, of tastes. The products are mortal, their producer is not. The author of corporeal forms is not corporeal, the one of sounds is not perceptible to the ear, the one of colours is not visible to the eye, the one of tastes is not perceived by taste. Apart from its infinity and immortality, the producer, the author (the Principle), is indeterminate, capable of becoming, in beings, yin or yang, active or passive, expanded or contracted, round or square, agent of life or of death, hot or cold, light or heavy, noble or vile, visible or invisible, black or yellow, bitter or sweet, perfumed or stinking. Deprived of all intellectual knowledge and of all intentional power, it knows all and can do all" (for it is immanent in all that which knows and is able, which is, says the commentary, supreme knowledge and power). (Lie Zi, chapter 1).

Dao cannot be possessed.

Shun asked Zheng, his prime minister. "Can one come to possess the Principle?" - Zheng replied. "Not possessing your own body, how can you aspire to possess the Principle?" – "If my body is not mine, whose is it?" asked Shun. – "Your body is a loan of gross matter, which heaven and earth have lent you for a time" said Zheng. "Your life is a transitory combination of subtle matter which you owe also to heaven and earth. Your destiny, your activity forms an integral part of the flux of beings under the action of heaven and earth. Your children and grandchildren are a renewal (literally, a change of skin) that heaven and earth have given you. You go forward in life without knowing what pushes you, you eat without knowing how you assimilate; the powerful and unknowable action of heaven and earth moves you in everything; and you wish to appropriate something to yourself?" (Zhuang Zi, ch. 22).

Dao cannot be situated.

Dong Guo Zi said to Zhuang Zi: "Where is Dao"? "Everywhere", said Zhuang Zi. "For example" asked Dong Guo Zi, "For example in this blade of grass". "And lower"? "It is in this fragment of tile." "And lower?" "In this piss and shit," said Zhuang Zi. Dong

Guo Zi asked no further. Then Zhuang Zi took up the conversation and said to him. "Master, questioning like that will get you nowhere. Such a procedure is too imperfect. It is like that of the market experts who summarily judge the fatness of a pig by pressing a foot on it (the depth of the imprint indicating how fat or lean is the pig). Do not ask if Dao is in this or that, it is in all things. That is why it is given the epithets great, supreme, complete, universal, and total. All these different terms apply to one and the same reality, to the cosmic unity. Let us transport ourselves in spirit, beyond the universe of dimensions and places, and there is no longer a question of situating Dao. Let us transport ourselves outside the world of activity, into the realm of inaction, indifference, rest, the void, simplicity, leisure and harmony, and there will no longer be a question of wishing to qualify the Principle. It is the indeterminate infinite. It is a waste of time wishing to reach it, to situate it and to study its movements. No science goes that far. Dao, the Principle which has caused all beings to be beings, is not itself subject to the same laws as beings. The Principle which has caused all beings to be limited is itself unlimited, infinite. It is therefore stupid to ask where it may be found. As for evolution and its phases, fullness and emptiness, prosperity and decadence, the Principle produces this succession, but is not this succession. It is the author of causes and effects, but not the causes and effects. It is the author of condensations and dissipations (births and deaths), but it is not itself condensation or dissipation. Everything comes from it, and evolves by and under its influence. It is in all beings through a termination of the norm; but it is not identical with beings since it is neither differentiated nor limited." (Zhuang Zi, chapter 22).

Dao is known by abstraction.

Purity said to infinity: "Do you know the Principle?" "I do not know it" said Infinity. Then Purity said to Inaction: "Do you know the Principle?" "I know it" said Inaction. "By reflection or intuition?" asked Purity. "By reflection" said Inaction. – "Explain yourself" said purity. "It is like this," said Inaction. "I think that the Principle is the confluence of contrasts, nobility and baseness, collection and dispersion. I know it therefore by reflection." Purity went along to consult the Primordial State. "Which one replied best," he asked. "Who was right and who was wrong." The Primordial State said: "Infinity said 'I do not know the Principle;' this reply is profound. Inaction said, 'I know the Principle;' this reply is superficial. Infinity was right to say that he knew nothing of the essence of the principle. Inaction was able to say that she knew it in its exterior manifestations." Struck by this reply, Purity said: "Ah, then not to know it is to know it (its essence), to know it (its manifestations) is not to know it (such as it is in reality). But how can one understand that it is through not knowing it that one knows it?" "It is like this" said the Primordial State. "Dao (the Principle) cannot be understood, what is understood is not it. The Principle cannot be seen, what is seen is not it. Can one conceive other than by reason (and not by imagination), the non-sentient being which has produced all sentient beings?

No, without a doubt! In consequence the Principle which is this non-sentient being, not being imaginable, cannot further be described. Remember this well. One who asks questions about the Principle, and one who replies, show both that they are ignorant of what the Principle is. One cannot ask nor reply concerning what the Principle is. These are vain questions, inept replies, which imply that those who make them are ignorant of what the universe is and what was the great origin. Such people will not elevate themselves beyond the earthly heights of the Kun Lun Mountains; they will not reach the absolute void of perfect abstraction. (Zhuang Zi, chapter 22).

Diffuse Light asked Formless (the infinite, indeterminate being, Dao, the Principle): "Do you exist, or do you not?" She heard no reply. Having stared for a long time, she only saw an obscure void, in which despite all efforts she could distinguish nothing, could perceive nothing and could grasp nothing. "This is the highest" she said; "it is impossible to inquire about this state. Ideas of being and nothingness are current. Non-being cannot be conceived of as existing. But here, existing is Formless (the infinite, indeterminate being). This is the supreme height; it is the Principle." (Zhuang Zi, chapter 22).

Knowledge went north as far as the Black sea and climbed the Mountain of Obscurity, where she met Inaction. Knowledge said to Inaction: "I have something to ask you. How can one come to know Dao? What position should one take, and what should one do to understand it? Where should one start and which way should one go in order to reach it?" Inaction did not reply to these three questions; not because she did not wish to reply, but because, in truth, she did not know how to reply. Obtaining no reply, Knowledge went as far as the White Sea and climbed the Mountain of Investigation where she saw Abstraction and asked her these same three questions. "Ah!" said Abstraction, "I will tell you," but just as she was going to speak she forgot what it was all about. Disappointed, Knowledge went to the Imperial Palace and put these questions to the Yellow Emperor. The latter said to her. "In order to know Dao, it is above all necessary not to think or reflect; to understand it no position should be taken and nothing must be done. To reach it one should begin at no precise point and one should follow no fixed way." "Well!" said Knowledge, "from amongst them and us, who acted the best?" "Inaction" said the Yellow Emperor, "because she said nothing at all. Then Abstraction, who barely spoke about it. We two were wrong in speaking. The saying goes: 'He who knows does not speak (because he knows he cannot explain what he knows); he who speaks shows that he does not know.'" The Sage does not speak, even in order to teach. Dao cannot be reached and its action cannot be grasped. All that which may be taught and learnt, such as goodness, fairness, rites; all such things are after and inferior to the Principle; these things were only invented when the true notion of the Principle and its action was lost, at the beginning of the decadence. (Zhuang Zi, chapter 22).

It is in abstraction that one must look for the Principle. It is from the infinite that one must look at particular beings. Nowadays the majority of men do the opposite. Philosophers lose themselves in their speculations, sophists in their distinctions and seekers in their investigations. All these are captive within the limits of space, blinded by particular things. The peasant is absorbed by his work, the businessman by business, the craftsman by his craft, and the common people by the small affairs of each day. The more the circumstances are favourable, the more they submerge themselves in their speciality. At each setback, at each deception, they are afflicted. They follow a fixed idea, without ever accommodating themselves to things. They overwork their bodies and overwhelm their minds. And they do that all their lives, alas! (Zhuang Zi, ch. 24).

Man whose body occupies such a small space on earth, traverses space as far as heaven by his spirit. He knows the great unity, his first state of concentration, the prolificity of beings, universal evolution, the immensity of the world, the reality of all that it contains; the steadfastness of the laws that rule it. At the base of everything is nature. In nature's profound depths is the pivot of all (Dao, the Principle) which seems to be double (yin and yang) without really being so, and which is knowable, but inadequately. Man comes to know it through force of seeking it. Extending itself beyond the limits of the world, his spirit reaches the ungraspable reality (the Principle) which is always the same, always without default. That is his greatest success. He obtains it through reasoning, following the certainties already acquired, on to things still uncertain, which become little by little certain in their turn, knowledge of the Principle being the final supreme certitude. (Zhuang Zi, chapter 24).

The Yellow Emperor reigned for fifteen years, delighting in his popularity, preoccupied with his health, indulging his senses, to the point where he became emaciated and haggard. When he had reigned for thirty years, making continual intellectual and physical efforts to organize the empire and ameliorate the lot of the people, he found himself to be even thinner and more worn out. Then he said to himself, sighing: I must have gone too far. If I am unable to do good to myself, how can I do any good to all. Having said that, he gave up the cares of government, left the palace, sent away his entourage, and deprived himself of all music. He reduced himself to an ordinary frugal state and shut himself in a remote apartment where, for three months, he applied himself solely to regulating his thoughts and controlling his body. One day during this seclusion, whilst taking his siesta, he dreamt that he was walking in the land of Hua Xu. This land is to the west of Yen Zhou and to the north of Tai Zhou at I don't know how great a distance from this land of Qi. One can go there neither by boat nor in a carriage; only the flight of the soul can reach it. In that land there is no chief, and everything happens spontaneously. The people have neither desires nor lust, but only their natural instincts. No one loves life nor fears death; they all live to their allotted term. There are no friendships or hatreds, no gains or losses, no interests and no fears. Water does not drown them, fire does not burn them. No weapon can wound them, no hand can harm them. They mount into the air as though they are climbing steps, and they stretch themselves out in space as though on a bed. Clouds and mists do not hinder their sight; the noise of thunder does not affect their hearing. Neither beauty nor ugliness moves their hearts and no height or depth upsets their course. The flight of their souls takes them everywhere. On his awakening, a peaceful light shone within him. He called his principal ministers, Tian Lao, Li Mu, Tai Shan Ji, and said to them: "During three months of retreat I have controlled my mind and subdued my body, thinking how I should govern without wearing myself out. I did not find the solution during the waking state; it came to me whilst I was asleep. I know now that the supreme Principle is not reached by positive efforts (but through abstraction and inaction). The light shines within me but I cannot explain it any further to you." (Lie Zi, chapter 2).

Dao is the author, motor, pivot, universal norm.

The Principle produces in abundance, but without filling itself up.

Empty abyss, it seems to be (is) the ancestor (origin) of all beings.

It is peaceful, simple, modest and amiable.

Spilling itself out in waves, it seems to remain (it remains) always the same.

I do not know of whom it is the child (where it comes from). It seems to have been (it was) before the Sovereign. (Lao Zi, chapter 4).

(The commentaries on the above chapter may be summarized as follows: This important chapter is devoted to the description of Dao, the Principle. Because of the abstraction of the subject, and perhaps also through prudence, his conclusions shocking the ancient Chinese, Lao Zi uses three times the verb 'to seem' instead of the categorical verb 'to be'. Dao, in itself is like an immense abyss, like an infinite spring. All sentient beings are produced by its exteriorization, through its action or virtue operating in the heaven-earth binomial. But sentient beings, terminations of the Principle, do not add to the Principle, do not make it greater and do not fill it up. Since they do not go outside it, they neither diminish it nor empty it, and the Principle always remains the same. Four qualities are attributed to it, which later on will be put forward for imitation by the sage. These qualities are inadequately translated by the positive terms, peaceful, simple, modest and amiable. The terms of the Chinese text are in fact more complex: Being soft without sharp corners or cutting edges; not being embroiled or complicated; not dazzling but shining with a tempered, somewhat dull light; willingly sharing the dust, the humbleness of the common people).

Master Kui, also known as Nan Bo, asked Nu Yu: "How is it that, despite your great age, you have the freshness of a child?" "Because I have lived in conformity with the doctrine of the Principle, and have not worn myself out," said Nu Yu. "Could I learn this doctrine?" asked Master Kui. "You don't have what it takes," replied Nu Yu. "Bu Liang Yi had what it needed. I taught it to him. After three days he had forgotten the outside world. Seven days more and he had lost the notion of the objects which surrounded him. Nine days more and he had lost the notion of his own existence. He then acquired clear penetration, and through it the science of momentary existence in the uninterrupted chain. Having acquired this knowledge he ceased to distinguish the past from the present and the future, and life from death. He understood that in reality killing did not cause death, engendering did not cause birth, the Principle sustaining the being across its becomings and endings. It is therefore justly called the permanent fixer. It is from it, the fixed, that all mutations come." "Did you invent this doctrine?" asked Master Kui. "No!" said Nu Yu, "I learnt it from the son of Fu Mei, disciple of Lao Song's little son, disciple of Zhan Ming, disciple of Nie Xu, disciple of Su Yi, disciple of Yu Nou, disciple of Huan Ming, disciple of San Liao, disciple of Yi Shi." (The commentary says: Are these the names of men [or does this indicate an initiatic chain?] It is possible, but these words can also be interpreted as meaning: "I have not drawn this doctrine from my imagination. I have discovered it by meditating on the mystery of the origin.") (Zhuang Zi, chapter 6.)

Heaven and earth, so majestic, are dumb. The course of the stars and seasons, so regular, is not deliberate. The evolution of beings follows an immanent, non-formulated law. Imitating these models, the superior being, the true sage, does not intervene, does not act, but lets everything follow its course. The transcendent heaven-earth binomial presides over all transformations, the succession of lives and deaths, the mutations of all beings, without any of these beings having an explicit knowledge of the first cause of all these movements, of Dao the Principle which makes everything persist since the beginning. The immensity of space is the go-between of heaven and earth. The least straw owes its existence to heaven and earth. Heaven and earth preside over the continual evolution of beings, which time after time are raised up or put down; over the regular rotation of the yin and the yang, of the four seasons, etc. From amongst beings, some seem to disappear, but continue nevertheless to exist; others, through having lost their bodies, only become more transcendent. Heaven and earth nourish all beings without their knowing it. From this idea of the universe, we can go back to the confused knowledge of its cause, Dao, the Principle. This is the only way. One can say of the Principle only that it is the origin of everything, that it influences everything whilst remaining indifferent. (Zhuang Zi, chapter 22).

The unique universal principle subsists in the multiplicity of beings, in their beginnings and endings. All distinct beings are such as they are through accidental and temporary differentiation (individuation) from the whole and their destiny is to return again into this whole, of which their essence is a participant. Of this return, the common people say that the living that have died and do not find their way, wander as phantoms; and that those who have died and found the way, are defunct (extinguished). Survival, extinction, these are two ways of speaking of an identical return, which comes from their having applied notions proper to sentient beings, to the state of being non-sentient. The truth is that, come out by their emergence from formlessness (the indeterminate being), returned by their death into formlessness, beings retain a reality (that of the universal whole) but they have no longer a place; they keep a duration (that of the eternal whole) but they no longer have time. Reality without place, duration without time, is the universe, the cosmic unity, the whole, the Principle. It is in the bosom of this unity, that births and deaths, appearances and disappearances, are produced, silently and imperceptibly. They have called it the heavenly gate or the natural gate, the gateway of entrance and exit of existence. This gate is the non-being of form, the indefinite being. Everything comes out from it. The sentient being cannot be, in the last instance, the issue of the sentient being. It is necessarily issued from the non-being of form. This non-being of form is unity, the Principle. This is the secret of the sages, the kernel of esoteric science. In their dissertations on the origin, those of the ancients who had reached a superior degree of knowledge expressed three opinions. Some thought that the definite, infinite being, author of all limited beings, existed from all eternity. Others, doing away with the infinite being, thought that limited beings existed from all eternity, passing through alternating phases of life and death. Others, finally, thought that formlessness (the indefinite, infinite being) was first of all, and from it emanated all the finite beings, with their births and deaths. Indefinite being, birth, death; these three terms hold together like the head, body, and tail of an animal. I (Zhuang Zi) support this thesis. For me, the indefinite being, all births, all deaths, form a complex, a whole. I shake hands with those who think the same. However, strictly speaking, the three opinions stated above can be reconciled. They are related like the branches of one and the same tree. The particular being is to the indefinite being, what the soot (palpable deposit) is to the (impalpable) smoke. When the soot is deposited, there has been no new production, but only a passage from the impalpable to the palpable, soot being concrete smoke. And likewise, if this soot is dissipated in smoke, there will again only have been a conversion, without essential modification. I know that the term conversion, which I employ in order to express the succession of lives and deaths in the bosom of the Principle, is not in common usage; but I must speak thus, under pain of not being able to express myself at all. The disjointed members of a sacrificed cow are a victim. Several rooms are a house. Life and death are a same state. From life to death, there is no transformation; there is a conversion. Philosophers become heated when it comes to defining the difference between these two states. For me, there is no difference; the two states are only one.

When one hurts someone, the closer that person is to one, the less one makes excuses. One asks pardon of a peasant stranger whose foot one has stepped on; but the father does not apologise to his son in the same situation. The highest of rites, is not to perform them. The highest expedience is to laugh at everything. The height of intelligence is to think of nothing. The height of sincerity is not to pay deposits. It is necessary to curb the digressions of appetite, correct the aberrations of the mind, and push aside all that hinders the free inflowing of the Principle. Wishing to be noble, rich, distinguished, respected, renowned, endowed, makes up the six appetites; appearance, deportment, breathing and thought cause mental aberrations. Antipathy, sympathy, complacency, anger, sadness, joy, hinder the free inflowing of the Principle. Repulsion and attraction, give and take, knowledge and ability, are so many obstacles. The inside from which these twenty-four causes of disorder have been eliminated, becomes regulated, calm, luminous, empty, non-acting and capable of all things. The Principle is the source of all active faculties, life is their manifestation, individual nature is a modality of this life, its movements are the acts; wasted acts are its faults. The learned devise and speculate; and, when they are unable to see more clearly, they act like little children and stare at an object. Orderly action is acting only when one cannot do otherwise. Acting without being obliged to do so, is hazardous interference. Knowing and acting must go hand in hand. (Zhuang Zi, chapter 23).

All beings are contained in Dao, the Principle, are one with the Principle, in which their mutations do not cause any change. Let us take a round basin, of no great depth, full of water, in the middle of which a pebble is placed.

Small fish swim along the edge of the basin, always in a circle around the pebble. Their movement has no point of origin, and no fixed end. They go round and round, and nothing changes; neither the basin, nor the water, nor they; and the movement they give themselves causes no change in the complex whole. Thus it is with all the beings in the Principle. (Guan Yin. Zi).

Dao embraces the entire universe, that which has form and that which is without form, that which is subtle and that which is gross, heaven and earth, sun, moon and stars, the yin and the yang. It is the pivot of all. It is the source from which all that is has flowed. It is eternal, without morning or evening. It is darkness and light, power and inertia, strength and weakness, incommensurable height and unfathomable depth. It is equally both in the infinitely great and the infinitely small. It shines in the sun and the moon, it walks in the quadrupeds and it flies in the birds. It outflanks the universe; it concentrates itself in a straw. It establishes universal unity and harmony by enclosing in its bosom myriads of contrasts and contradictions. (Huai Nan Zi).

The sage understands that, linked together one with the other, all beings form a body (a whole), but he does not seek to penetrate the intimate nature of this link, which is the mystery of the cosmic norm. Following the universal law in all his movements, he is the agent of heaven. Men call him a sage, because he cooperates with heaven. He is not preoccupied with knowing what cannot be known, but acts with the knowledge that he has, in perseverance. He does not reflect on the qualities he may have, but leaves the job of ascertaining them to others, not attributing the gift of nature to himself. He is benevolent towards men, not from affection, but by instinct, and he does not need their recognition. (Zhuang Zi, chapter 25)

Dao acts without acting.

The Principle does not claim any title (Lord, Governor). It does not act. Doing nothing, there is nothing it cannot do (not by intervening actively, but as the evolutionary norm contained in everything). In appearance, to our human manner of seeing, times succeed one another; the universe is changing, adversity and prosperity alternate. In reality, these variations, effects of a unique norm, do not modify the immutable whole. All contrasts find a place in this whole without disturbance; just as all kinds of plants grow together in a swamp, or trees and rocks are mingled on a mountain. (Zhuang Zi, chapter 25).

The origin of the universe.

'Above all, is the Principle, common to all, containing and penetrating everything, whose proper attribute and sole designation is infinity, for it has no name of its own.' said Tai Gong Diao to Shao Zi. Then the latter said to him, 'explain how all that which is comes from this infinity.' Tai Gong Diao said: 'Emanated from the Principle, the yin and the yang influence each other, destroy each other, and reproduce themselves reciprocally. From this comes the physical world, with the succession of seasons, which are produced and destroyed by one another. From this comes the moral world, with its attractions and repulsions, loves and hates; thence the distinction of the sexes, and their union for procreation; then certain correlative and successive states, such as prosperity and adversity, security and danger. Then abstract ideas of mutual influence, of reciprocal causality, of a certain circular evolution in which beginnings follow endings. That is more or less what, drawn from observation and expressed in words, constitutes the sum of human knowledge. Those who know the Principle do not scrutinize further, they do not speculate either on the nature of the primordial emanation or the eventual end of the order of existing things.' Shao Zhi continued his questioning: 'Daoist authors have, however, discussed these questions. Thus Ji Zhen holds to a passive and unconscious emanation, Jie Zi to an active and conscious production. Which one is right?' 'Tell me,' said Tai Gong Diao, 'why do cocks go cock-a-doodle-doo, why do dogs go bow-wow? The fact of this difference is known to everyone, but the wisest will never tell you why. It is the same with nature; that is all we know of it. Attenuate an object until it becomes invisible, amplify it until it becomes incomprehensible, you will not extract its reason for being from it. And how much less will you ever bring to light the question of the genesis of the universe, the most abstruse question of all? "It is the work of an author," said Jie Zi. "It became out of nothing," said Ji Zhen. Neither of these two will ever prove their words. Both of them are in error. It is impossible that the universe had a pre-existing author.

It is impossible for being to have come from nothingness. Man can know nothing about his own life, because the law that rules life and death, his own transformations, escapes him; what can he know therefore of the law ruling the great cosmic transformations, universal evolution? To say of the universe "someone has made it" or "it came out of nothing," these are not demonstrable propositions, but gratuitous suppositions. For me, when I look back towards the origin, I see it losing itself in a far distant infinity; when I look in front towards the future, I do not catch a glimpse of any end. Now human words are not able to express what is infinite, that which has no end. Limited like the beings that use them, they can only express the affairs of the limited world of these beings, limited and changing things. They cannot be applied to the Principle, which is infinite, immutable, and eternal. Now, after the emanation, the Principle from which beings emanate, being itself inherent in these beings, cannot properly be called the author of these beings; this refutes Jie Zi. As the Principle inherent in all beings existed before beings, one cannot strictly say that these beings have come out of nothing; this refutes Ji Zhen. When one now says the Principle, this term no longer designates the solitary being, such as it was in primordial times; it designates the being that exists in all beings, the universal norm which presides over cosmic evolution. The nature of the Principle, the nature of being, is incomprehensible and ineffable. Only the limited can be understood and expressed. The Principle acts as the pole, as the axis, for the universality of beings, and we say of it only that it is the pole, the axis of universal evolution, without attempting either to understand it or explain it.' (Zhuang Zi, ch. 25.)

The sea, image of the Principle.

Zhun Mang was going towards the eastern ocean when he met Yuan Feng, who said to him: "Master, where are you going?" "To the sea" said Zhun Mang. "Why?" asked Yuan Feng. "Because it is the image of the Principle" said Zhun Mang. "All the rivers run into it without filling it. Water leaves it without emptying it; just as things come out of the Principle and return to it. That is why I am going to the sea." (Zhuang Zi, chapter 12.)

The universal mother.

The expansive transcendental power which resides in the median space, the virtue of the Principle, does not die. It is always the same and acts the same, without diminution or cessation.

This virtue is the mysterious mother of all beings.

The doorway of this mysterious mother is the root of heaven and earth, Dao, the Principle.

Sprouting forth, she does not expend herself; acting, she does not tire herself. (Lao Zi, chapter 6).

(The commentaries on the above chapter explain that the term doorway, with the impression of two swinging doors, signifies the alternating movement, the play of yin and yang, first modification of the Principle. This play was the root that is to say it produced heaven and earth).

4. DE, THE ACTION, OR VIRTUE, OF DAO.

The bellows:

The betwixt of heaven and earth, seat of Dao the Principle, the place from where *de*, its virtue, acts, is like a bellows, like the bag of a bellows of which heaven and earth would be the two boards, which empties itself without exhausting itself, which moves itself eternally without cease. (Lao Zi, chapter 5).

The unwinding:

This being, Dao the Principle, is not light above and dark below, as are opaque material bodies. Like a slender thread, it unwinds itself (as continuous existence and action). It has no name of its own. It goes back to the time when there were no other beings but it. It has no parts; from in front one sees no head, from behind no rear.

It is this primordial Principle that has ruled, and rules, all beings right up to the present. Everything that has been, or is, since the ancient origin, is from the unwinding of the Principle. (Lao Zi, chapter 14).

(The commentaries on the above chapter say that *de*, the continuous and varying action of Dao, is picturesquely described using the metaphor *ji,* the unwinding of a spool. The meaning is clear. The diverse products of the Principle are manifestations of *de,* its virtue; the indefinite chain of these manifestations of the Principle can be called its unwinding).

All of the beings which play a rôle in the great manifestation of the cosmic theatre have come from the Principle, through its action or virtue (through its unwinding). (Lao Zi, chapter 21).

The great Principle extends itself in all directions. It lends itself willingly to the genesis of all beings (its participants). When a work is accomplished, it does not attribute it to itself. It nourishes all beings with kindness without imposing itself on them as a master (for having nourished them; leaving them free; not exacting any degrading return from them). Because of its constant disinterestedness, one might think it would become diminished. This is not so. Every being to which it is so liberal, runs towards it. It therefore finds itself magnified (through this universal trust). Lao Zi, ch. 34).

The Heaven-Earth binomial.

The ancients considered the Principle in the heaven-earth binomial. It is from this binomial that they drew the natural ideas of goodness and fairness, (opposed to the artificial ideas of goodness and fairness of the Confucians); then the ideas of functions and office; and then those of capacity, responsibility, sanction etc. As abstract ideas increased, intellectuals were distinguished from imbeciles; then there were superior and inferior men. They were all treated according to their degree. The sages served the ruler, nurtured the foolish, amending them by example, without constraining them, like the action of heaven and earth. This was the era of absolute peace, of perfect government. No one made dissertations or quibbled about entities and denominations as do the sophists today. They did not try to reward or punish adequately every good or evil deed, as our legalists would like to. For every solution, they inquired into the root, the origin, the Principle which contains all; and it is this view from above that made the superiority of their government. Whereas through being lost in details, our sophists and legalists are good-for-nothing. (Zhuang Zi, chapter 13).

Confucius went to visit Lao Dan and found him sitting motionless, carried away in ecstasy. The transport had seized him whilst he was drying his hair, after his ablutions. Confucius waited discreetly until he came to, and then said: 'You had left things and people; you had withdrawn yourself into the isolation of the self.' 'Yes,' said Lao Dan. 'I was frolicking in the origin of things.' 'What does that mean?' asked Confucius. 'I have not yet fully recovered,' said Lao Dan; 'my tired mind is not yet free to think, my closed mouth can scarcely articulate; however I will try to satisfy you. When the two modalities of being are differentiated in the primordial being, their gyration begins, and cosmic evolution follows. The highest point of the yin (condensed in the earth) is peaceful passivity. The highest point of the yang (condensed into heaven) is fecund activity. The passivity of the earth offers itself to heaven, and heaven's activity acts on it, producing all beings. An invisible force, the action and reaction of the heaven-earth binomial, produces all evolution. Beginning and ending, fullness and emptiness, astronomical revolutions, phases of the sun and moon; these things are produced by the same unique cause, which no one sees, but which functions always. Life develops itself towards an end; death is a return towards a term. Beginnings succeed one another without cease, without one knowing the origin, without one seeing the end. The action and reaction of heaven and earth is the unique motor of this movement. In this is beauty, supreme joy. It is the lot of the superior man to frolic in this rapture.' 'But how may one reach that?' asked Confucius. 'Through absolute indifference,' replied Lao Dan. 'The animals that populate the steppes are not attracted by any particular pasture; the fish living in the water do not hold themselves to any fixed habitat; in consequence, no displacement upsets their peace. All beings form an immense whole. He who is united with this unity, even so far as to have lost the awareness of his personality, who considers his body as he considers dust, life and death as day and night; what is there that can move this man, for whom gain and loss, happiness and misfortune, are nothing? He despises ranks like mud because he knows more noble things than these. No vicissitude can touch one who has this nobility of self. Of all possible changes, none can alter his peace. He that has reached the Principle understands this.' 'Ah!' said Confucius amazed, 'here is a teaching as great as heaven and earth; can it be summed up in some formula, after the manner of the ancients?' Lao Dan replied: 'Springs well up naturally. The superior man is such spontaneously. Heaven is high, the earth is deep, and the sun and moon are luminous, all without formulae.' When he was outside, Confucius told all this to his disciple

Yen Hui. 'Until now,' he said, 'I have known as much about the Principle as the worms that live in vinegar. If the master had not lifted the veil covering my eyes, I would never have caught a glimpse of the perfect complex of heaven and earth' (the great cosmic unity). (Zhuang Zi, ch. 21).

The expansion of de:

At the great beginning, there was formlessness, the imperceptible being; there was no sentient being, and in consequence no name. The first being was non-sentient, the One, Dao, the Principle. The norm, the virtue emanating from the One, which gives birth to all beings, is called *de*. Multiplying itself without end, this participating virtue is called, in each one, *ming*, its share, lot or destiny. It is through alternating concentration and expansion that the norm gives birth to beings. In the being which is born, certain definite lines specify its bodily form. This bodily form contains the vital spirit. Each being has its way of acting, which constitutes its own nature. That is how beings descend from the Principle. They return through mental and moral Daoist culture, which brings individual nature back to conformity with the universal acting virtue, and the particular being to union with Dao, the Primordial Principle, the Great Void, the Great Whole. This return, this union, is achieved not through action but cessation; just as a bird closes its beak, stops singing, and is silent; a silent fusion with heaven and earth, in an apathy which seems stupid to those who understand nothing, but which is true mystical virtue, communion with the evolution of the cosmos. (Zhuang Zi, chapter 12).

A uniform transforming force emanates from the immense complex of heaven and earth; a unique law governs the mass of beings; a single ruler rules over a populous humanity. The ruler's power derives from the Principle; his person is chosen by heaven; so that he is referred to as mysterious, like the Principle. The rulers of antiquity abstained from all personal intervention, letting heaven govern through them. When Dao acts through the ruler, his ministers and officials; then all beings respond by absolute submission to this just and enlightened government. Above the universe the first Principle influences heaven and earth, which transmit this influence to all beings, making for good government in the human world and bringing out talents and abilities. Looked at another way, all prosperity comes from the government whose effectiveness derives from the Principle, through the intermediary of heaven and earth. That is why, when the ancient rulers desired nothing, there was abundance in the world; they did not act, and everything evolved; they remained deep in meditation, and the people lived in the most perfect order. The old saying sums this up: To one who is united with Unity, everything prospers; to one who has no personal interest, even the subtle beings are subjected. (Note: the traditional Chinese were haunted by nostalgia for the ancient times of peace and imperceptible government).

How true are these words of the Master! How great, how immense is the Principle which covers and supports all beings! The ruler should take great care to follow his inner sense! Natural action is heavenly action; the spontaneous verb is the heavenly influence; loving everyone and doing good to all beings is true goodness; fusing all differences into one is true greatness; not wishing to dominate others in any way is true breadth of spirit; possessing diverse things without dividing one's heart is true wealth; following the heavenly influence is the way to act; acting under this influence is acting effectively; serving as a docile intermediary of the Principle is perfection; not allowing one's determination to be affected by anything is constancy. The ruler should concentrate these six principles in himself, and then apply them to the government, and everything would follow its natural course. He should leave the gold in the rocks and the pearls in the depths, scorn wealth and honour and be indifferent to long life and early death. He should be neither vain in prosperity nor humiliated by adversity; he should disdain all the goods of this world, and he should not glorify himself because of his exaltation. His glory should be in understanding that all beings are a single universal complex, and that life and death are two modalities of the same being. (Zhuang Zi, chapter 12).

The universal norm.

There are no such things as distinct beings. There is only an 'I' by contrast with a 'he'. He and I are beings only of reason; there does not exist, in reality, this something closer which one calls mine, and this something further away which one calls yours. But who is the agent of this state of things, the motor of the great Whole? Everything happens as if there were a true governor, but whose nature cannot be understood. This hypothesis explaining phenomena is acceptable on condition that one does not make this governor a distinct material being. It is a tendency without palpable form, the norm inherent in the universe, its immanent evolutionary formula. Norms of all kinds, like those which make a body of several organs (the human soul is included here), a family of several persons, a state of numerous subjects, are so many participants of the universal governor. These participants neither augment nor diminish it, for they are communicated through it, not separated from it. Beings arise as prolongations of the universal norm. When a being ceases to exist, the norm remains. The norm of a being was before, and remains afterwards, unalterable and indestructible; the rest was only an appearance. It is from ignorance of this principle that have come all the pains and sorrows of man, the struggle for existence, fear of death, and apprehension of the mysteries beyond. This blindness is almost general, but not, however, universal. There are still men, few in number, who have not been seduced by the conventional traditionalism, who recognize no master but their reason, and who, through their meditations on the universe have deduced the doctrine expounded above. These men know that there is nothing real except the universal norm. The common people, unreflecting, believe in the real existence of everything. This modern error has drowned the ancient truth. It is so anchored, so inveterate, that the greatest sages in the eyes of the world, Yu the Great included, have been duped by it. To support the truth, I find myself almost alone." (Zhuang Zi, chapter 2.)

The yin and the Yang, two modalities.

When the Principle has emitted its virtue, the latter begins to evolve according to two alternating modalities. This evolution produces (or condenses) the median air (tenuous matter). From tenuous matter, under the influence of the two modalities yin and yang, all sentient beings are produced. Coming out from the yin (from strength) they pass to the yang (to the act), through the influence of the two modalities on matter. (Lao Zi, ch. 42.)

(In what follows, it is probably Zhuang Zi who speaks). He whose heart has reached the height of immutability emits a natural light (pure reason, with nothing conventional) which reveals to him what still remains of the artificial within. Then he rids himself of this artificiality and becomes stable. With time, the artificial disappears completely and only the natural remains. Men who have reached this state are called sons of heaven, heavenly people; that is to say they have returned to their natural state, become again what heaven had originally made them. This cannot be learnt either by theory or practice, but only by intuition or exclusion. To stop there, where one can learn no more, (and to hold oneself, says the commentary, in indifference and inaction) is to be perfectly wise. He who should try to pass beyond (deciding, acting, chancing) will be broken by the fatal course of things (for he will inevitably enter into conflict with destiny). When all

provisions have been made and all precautions taken for the maintenance of the body, when one has not provoked another by any offence, then, if some misfortune comes along, it must be attributed to destiny, not men, and in consequence one should take care not to avoid it by having recourse to some baseness, and take care likewise not to be saddened in one's heart. It is in the power of man to seal the tower of his spirit (his heart); he has the power to keep it sealed on condition that he neither examines nor discusses what is presented to it but simply refuses it access. Each act of he who is not yet perfectly indifferent, causes disorder. The object of the act penetrates his heart, is lodged there, and will come out of it no more. With each new act there is a new disorder. Whoever does evil in daylight will be punished by men; if done under cover of darkness, he will be punished by the shades. Reminding oneself that, when one is not observed by men, one is by invisible beings, makes for good behaviour, even in one's secret retreat. Those who fear for their lives do not struggle in order to become famous. Those who burn with acquisitiveness spread their activities outside. The first are men of reason, the second are businessmen. One sees these men raising themselves on tiptoe, hoisting themselves up, striving to succeed. They are storehouses of preoccupations and worries. They are so full of them, that there is no longer room in their hearts even for the love of their fellow beings. Therefore they are detested as being no longer men. Of all the instruments of death, desire is the most murderous; the famous Mo Ye sword has not killed as many men. The worst assassins are, they say, the yin and the yang, from whom no one escapes, out of all the people who populate the space between heaven and earth. And yet, in truth, if the yin and the yang kill them, it is because their appetites deliver them up to these assassins. (Zhuang Zi, 23.)

5. THE GREAT WHOLE

All is one, the cosmos:

At the time of Emperor Mu of the Zhou dynasty, a magician from the far west came to court. This man was able to pass unharmed through water or fire, pass through metal or stone without encountering any resistance, make torrents run backwards, change the position of town ramparts, levitate, or take on any form at will whilst keeping his human intelligence, and so on. Emperor Mu venerated him as a spirit, and served him as a disciple would serve his master, giving him the best he had of lodgings, food, and women. Yet the magician found the imperial palace uninhabitable, the imperial cuisine inedible, and the women of the harem unworthy of his affection. Then the emperor had a special palace built for him. The materials and workmanship were all exquisite. The expense used up the imperial treasure. The finished edifice reached a height of eight thousand feet. When the emperor dedicated it, he called it the Tower Reaching to Heaven. He filled it with selected young people called in from the Principalities of Zheng and Wei. He installed baths and a harem. He provided it with precious objects, fine silks, cosmetics, perfumes, and curiosities. He had the most famous symphonies performed there. Every month he provided new outfits of superb clothing, every day a profusion of exquisite things. None of this had any effect. The magician found nothing to his liking and lived without pleasure in his new lodging, from which he was frequently absent. The emperor was astonished by this, until one day during a festival, the magician said to him: "come with me." The emperor held on to the magician's wand which quickly lifted him up into space as far as the palace of transcendent men in the centre of heaven. This palace was made of gold and silver, ornamented with pearls and jade. It was situated above the region of the rain clouds, and seemed to float in space like a cloud. In this supraterrestrial world, sights, music, perfumes, tastes; nothing was as in the world of men. The emperor understood that he was in the city of the Sovereign on High. From up there, his earthly palace looked to him like a little pile of twigs and turf. He would have stayed there for years without even remembering his empire; but the magician invited him to follow him further. This time he took him up beyond the sun and moon, out of sight of land and oceans, into a blinding light, a deafening harmony. Seized with terror and vertigo, the emperor asked to go down. The descent was made with the rapidity of a meteorite falling through space. When he came to, the emperor found himself sitting on his seat, surrounded by his courtiers, his cup half full and his stew half eaten. "What happened to me?" he asked his entourage. "It seemed as if you had withdrawn yourself for an instant," they said. The emperor thought he had been away for at least three months. "How do you explain that?" he asked the magician. "Oh, nothing could be simpler," said the latter. "I took up your spirit, your body has not moved. Or, rather, I did not even displace your spirit, since all distinctions of time and place are illusory. The mental representation of all possibilities is made without movement and abstracted from time." It is from the time of this episode that the distaste of Emperor Mu for the government of his empire and the pleasures of his court began, and also his taste for wandering. It was then that, with his eight famous horses each of a different hue, he undertook his famous expedition beyond the western frontiers. He was accompanied by Zao Fu who drove his chariot, Qi He who served as groom and Shen Bai who drove the wagon assisted by Ben Rong. After having covered a thousand stages, he reached the Ju Sou tribe, who gave him swan's blood to drink and washed his feet with koumiss (two fortifiers). The following night was spent on the banks of the Red Torrent. The next day the emperor climbed Mount Kun Lun, visited the Yellow Emperor's ancient palace, and built a cairn in memory of his visit. Next he visited Xi Wang Mu, and was entertained by her near the Green Lake. They exchanged toasts, and the emperor did not hide the fact that it was painful for him to have to go back. After having contemplated the place where the sun rests at the end of its diurnal course of ten thousand stages, he made his way back to the empire. To sum up, he returned disillusioned, having found nothing that resembled his vision. "Alas!" he said sighing, "my posterity will say that I sacrificed duty to pleasure." And, in fact, having only looked for present happiness, he was not a good emperor and did not attain spiritual perfection, but only lived a long time, dying in his hundredth year. (Lie Zi, chapter 3.)

Lao Cheng Zi entered the school of Yin Wen (Guan Yin Zi) in order to learn the secret of the universal phantasmagoria. For three whole years the latter taught him nothing. Thinking from this coldness that his master judged him of little ability, Lao Cheng Zi excused himself and offered to withdraw. Master Yin Wen bowed to him (a mark of extraordinary esteem), led him to his room, and there, without witnesses (for the divulgence of esoteric knowledge), he said: "A long time ago, when Lao Dan left for the west, he summarised his doctrine for me in these words: 'The vital spirit and the material body are phantasmagoria. The words life and death designate the initial genesis of a being through the action of the generative virtue, and its final transformation under the influence of natural agents. The phantasmagoria is the succession of beginnings and transformations under the influence of the universal motor, until their number is complete. The Principle, first of the beings, is too mysterious, too profound, to be fathomed. We can only study corporeal becomings and endings, which are visible and manifest. Understanding that, practically, cosmic evolution consists of the succession of the two states of life and death; that is the key to the comprehension of the phantasmagoria. We are subject to this vicissitude, you and I, and we can observe its effects on ourselves.'" This teaching received, Lao Cheng Zi returned home, meditated on it for three months, and found the secret of the mystery. He penetrated it so well that he became master of life and death. He was able to modify the seasons, producing thunderstorms in winter and ice in summer. He was able to change birds into quadrupeds and vice-versa. He taught no one the formula, and no one has since recovered it. Moreover, says Lie Zi, those who seek the ability to transform things should keep it secret, and not make use of it. The ancient rulers did not owe their fame to extraordinary acts of science or courage. We know they preferred to act for the good of humanity, without ostentation. (Lie Zi, chapter 3).

Mental application has eight effects: action, deliberation, success, failure, happiness, sadness, life, and death; all of which belong to the body. Mental abstraction has six causes: Will, aversion, intense thought, sleep, delight, and terror; all of which belong to the mind. Those who do not know the natural origin of emotion preoccupy themselves with its cause when they experience it. Those who know that emotion has a natural origin no longer preoccupy themselves with it, because they know its cause. Everything in the body of a being, fullness and emptiness, gain and loss, is in harmony, in equilibrium, with the state of heaven and earth and the totality of beings which populate the cosmos. A predominance of yin makes one dream of fording a river, with a cool sensation. A predominance of yang makes one dream of passing through fire, with a burning sensation. A simultaneous excess of yin and yang makes one dream of risks and dangers, with fear and hope. In a state of satiety one dreams of giving; in a state of fast one dreams of taking. Superficial minds dream they are rising in the air, serious minds dream they are deep down in the water. Wearing a belt in bed makes one dream of snakes; seeing a plumed bird makes one dream of flying.

Before a bereavement one dreams of fire; before an illness one dreams of eating. After drinking a great deal one has sad dreams; after dancing too much one cries whilst dreaming. Lie Zi says: "A dream is a meeting made by the mind; reality (objective perception) is a contact with the body. Waking thoughts and sleeping dreams are equally impressions. Thus those of truly sound mind think and dream little, and attach little importance to their thoughts and dreams. They know that thoughts and dreams are not the reality they seem to be, but are reflections of the cosmic phantasmagoria. The ancient Sages did not think greatly when awake, did not dream when asleep, and they spoke neither of their thoughts nor their dreams because they believed as little in the one as the other." — In the south-eastern corner of the square earth is a land whose frontiers I do not know. It is called Gu Mang. The alternations of yin and yang do not make themselves felt, and there are no seasons; the sun and moon do not shine there, and there is neither day nor night. Its inhabitants do not eat, and do not wear clothes. They sleep almost continuously, awaking once every fifty days. They take as real what they have experienced during their sleep, and as illusion what they experience whilst awake. In the centre of the earth and of the four seas is the middle kingdom (China), set by the Yellow River, extending from the land of Yue as far as Mount Tai, with an east-west breadth of more than ten thousand stages. The alternations of yin and yang there produce hot and cold seasons; light and darkness alternate producing day and night. Amongst its inhabitants there are wise men and fools. Its natural and industrial products are numerous and varied. It has its princes, officials, rites, and laws. People talk and act there a great deal. They wake and sleep alternately, taking as real what they experience during the waking state, and as vain what they experience during sleep. In the north-west corner of the square earth is the land of Fu Lao where the ground, burnt without cease by the sun's rays, does not produce any cereals. The people live on fruit and roots which they eat raw. Brutal, they prize force more than justice. They are almost always moving and seldom rest. They are awake most of the time, and sleep little. They hold as real what they experience during the waking state. (Note the foregoing are fictitious states invented to make a point). (Lie Zi, chapter 3.)

Let us suppose now a man completely absorbed in the immense cosmic gyration, and moving with it in the infinite. He will no longer depend on anything. He will be perfectly free, in the sense that his person and his action will be united with the person and action of the great Whole. Thus one can say justly: "The superior man has no longer a self of his own; transcendent man has no action of his own; the Sage has not even a name of his own for he is one with the great Whole." (Zhuang Zi, chapter 1.)

The alternation of life and death is predetermined by heaven, like that of day and night. If a man submits himself stoically to fate, then nothing can happen against his will. If something happens which wounds him, it is because he has conceived affection for some being.

Should he love nothing, then he would be invulnerable. There are sentiments more elevated than the loves that are reputed to be noble. Thus, instead of loving heaven as a father he venerates it as a universal fact, and in place of loving his prince, even as far as dying for him, he sacrifices himself for the sole abstract notion of absolute devotion. When the streams dry up, the fish come together seeking to keep themselves moist by pressing against each other; and men admire this mutual charity! Would it not have been better if, earlier, they had each sought salvation in the deeper waters? Instead of always citing as examples the goodness of Yao and the malice of Jie, would men not be better off forgetting these two persons and orientating their morality towards the abstract perfection of the Principle? My body makes up a part of the great mass (of the cosmos, of nature, of the whole). In it lies the sustenance of my childhood, the activity of my maturity, peace in my old age, and rest in my death. It has been good to me during my life and it will be good to me during the state of death. From any particular place, an object put there may be stolen; but an object entrusted to the whole itself cannot be taken away. Identify yourself with the great mass; in it there is permanence; a permanence which is not motionless. There is a chain of transformations, with the self persisting through mutations without end. This time I am happy to be in a human form. I have already experienced in the past, and will experience in the future, the same contentment of being in an unlimited succession of diverse forms. Then why should I hate death, the beginning of my next contentment? The sage devotes himself to everything in which he takes part, which contains him, and in which he evolves. Abandoning himself to the thread of this evolution, he smiles at premature death, at excess old age, at the beginning and at the end. He smiles and wishes one to smile at all the vicissitudes of life; for he knows that all beings are part of the whole which evolves. (Zhuang Zi, chapter 6).

Union with the whole:

An official from Chen who was on a mission to the Principality of Lu, met a certain Shu Sun who said: "We have a Sage here in Lu." "You don't mean Kong Qiu?" (Confucius), said the official. "Yes!" said Shu Sun. "How do you know he is truly a Sage?" asked the official. "Because I have heard his disciple Yen Hui say that Kong Qiu thinks with his body" said Shu Sun. "Then," said the official, "we also have a Sage, Geng Sang Zi, a disciple of Lao Dan, who sees with his ears and hears with his eyes." This remark of the official from Chen reached the ears of the Prince of Lu, who, most intrigued, sent a high-ranking minister bearing rich presents to invite Geng Sang Zi to his court. Geng Sang Zi accepted the invitation, and was received by the prince with great respect. Straight away Geng Sang Zi said to him: "You have been misinformed about my seeing with my ears and hearing with my eyes; one organ cannot be used as another." "That does not matter," said the prince, "I wish to know your doctrine." "It is this," said Geng Sang Zi; "my body is intimately united with my mind; my mind and body are intimately united with the force and matter of the cosmos, which are intimately united with the primordial formlessness, the indefinite infinite being, the Principle. In consequence of this intimate union, every consonance and dissonance which occurs in the universal harmony, be it close or at a great distance, is perceived by me, but in such a way that I cannot say through which organ I perceive it. I know without knowing how I come to know." (Lie Zi, chapter 4. — The commentary says that this is perfect Daoist knowledge; the consonance of two instruments tuned to the same note; the cosmos and the individual, perceived through intimate, total, sense).

The Yellow Emperor had reigned for nineteen years and his orders were obeyed throughout the empire, when he heard of Master Guang Cheng, who lived on Mount Kong Tong. He sought him out and addressed him with the following words: "I have heard tell, Master, that you have reached the supreme Principle. I venture to ask you to communicate its quintessence to me. I will use it for making good cereal harvests to feed the people. I will regulate the temperature for the benefit of all living beings. Give me the formula, please." Master Guang Cheng replied: 'You push ambition even so far as wishing to lord it over nature. To entrust its forces to you would be to the loss of all beings. Passionate man, if you were to govern the world, you would want it to rain before the clouds were formed, you would make the leaves fall whilst still green; the sun and the moon would soon be extinguished. Conceited and egoistic being, what can you have in common with the supreme Principle?' The Yellow

Emperor returned home confused, gave up his government, and lived in a makeshift hut with a straw mat as his sole furnishing. After spending three months in this retreat, reflecting and meditating, he went back to Master Guang Cheng whom he found lying with his head towards the north (looking south, the position of a teacher). Taking the place of a pupil, quite humbly, the Yellow Emperor approached on his knees, prostrated himself, touching the ground with his forehead, and said: "I know, Master, that you have reached the supreme Principle. Will you teach me how to conduct and conserve myself?" "Well put, this time," said Master Guang Cheng. "Come closer, I am going to reveal the basis of the Principle to you. Its essence is mystery; it is obscurity, indistinctness, silence. When one looks at nothing, listens to nothing, envelops one's spirit in withdrawal, the matter of the body becomes spontaneously right. Be withdrawn, detached, don't wear out your body or rouse your instincts and you can last forever. When your eyes no longer look at anything, when your ears no longer listen to anything, when your heart (intelligence and will) knows and desires nothing more, when your spirit has enveloped and in a sense absorbed your matter, then this matter (your body) will last forever. Take care of your interior, defend your exterior. Wishing to learn many things is what wears one out. Follow me in spirit, beyond the light as far as the principle yang of all splendour; and beyond the darkness as far as the principle yin of darkness. Follow me now, beyond these two principles, as far as unity (the supreme Principle) which rules over heaven and earth, which contains in germ, and from which emanate, the yin and the yang, and all beings. Knowing this Principle is the great science which does not wear one out. Holding oneself at rest in its contemplation is what makes one last forever. Any being who conserves himself, keeps his vigour. I myself have embraced unity; I am established in universal harmony. I have now lived twelve hundred years and my body is not weakened." "Heavenly being!" said the Yellow Emperor, touching his forehead on the ground. "Listen without interrupting," said Master Guang Cheng. "The first Principle is essentially infinite and unfathomable; men use in error, when speaking of it, the terms "end" and "highest." Those who knew it became the emperors and kings of the heroic age and ended by becoming gods." Those who did not know it remained terrestrial beings, ignorant and sensual. Nowadays the first Principle is so forgotten that all beings leaving the earth return to it. I also shall stay no longer in this world. I leave you, to go beyond the gate of the infinite, to saunter in immeasurable spaces. I am going to unite my light with that of the sun and the moon; I am going to fuse my duration with that of heaven and earth. I don't even wish to know if men think as I do, or differently. When they are all dead, I will survive, having alone, in these decadent times, reached union with unity." Zhuang Zi, chapter 11.)

The politician Yun Jiang, who was wandering in the east, beyond the Fu Yao River, unexpectedly met the immortal Hong Meng, who was hopping along, beating out a rhythm on his thighs. (Daoist immortals are almost always shown in eccentric posture, a sign of their contempt for ordinary life.) Surprised, Yun Jiang stopped, assumed the ritual posture, and said to him: "Venerable one, who are you? What are you doing there?" Without ceasing to hop, and tap on his thighs, Hong Meng replied: "I am taking a walk." Convinced that he was dealing with a transcendent being, Yun Jiang said: "I would like to ask you a question." "Bah!" said Hong Meng. "Yes!" said Yun Jiang. "The heavenly influx is upset, the earthly one is hindered; the six emanations are obstructed, the four seasons are deranged. I would like to put order back into the universe, for the good of the beings that inhabit it. Will you tell me how?" "I don't know, I don't know," said Hong Meng, shaking his head, slapping his sides, and hopping. Yun Jiang could get no further. Three years later, when he was wandering once more beyond the plain of You Song in the east, Yun Jiang again unexpectedly met Hong Meng. Full of joy, he ran towards him, and reached him saying: "Heavenly being, do you still remember me?" Then, prostrating himself twice and bowing his head, he added: "I wish to ask you a question." "What can I teach you?" said Hong Meng; "I who walk without knowing why, who wander without knowing where I am going; I who only saunter about without being occupied with anything, so as to avoid being annoyed by any untimely interference." "I also would like, as you, to wander free and without worries; but people follow me everywhere I go; it is real slavery; they have just let me go and I profit from this respite to question you," said Yun Jiang. "Poor man!" said Hong Meng; "what can I say to you, involved as you are with the government of men? Who troubles the empire, does violence to nature, and hinders the action of heaven and earth? Who upsets the animals, troubles the sleep of the birds, and annoys even the plants and the insects; who acts thus, if it is not the politician with his systems for governing the people?" "Is that how you judge me?" said Yun Jiang. "I have gone to much trouble to find you; I beg you to teach me." "Actually you have great need to learn," said Hong Meng. "Listen, therefore. Begin by intervening in nothing, and everything will naturally follow its course. Get rid of your personality (literally, let your body fall off like clothing), give up the use of your senses, forget relationships and contingencies, drown yourself in the great whole; rid yourself of your will and intelligence, annihilate yourself by abstraction even as far as no longer having a soul. What's the good of speculating, since the unconscious is the universal law? The mass of beings return unconsciously to their origin, and he who spends his life in unconsciousness, follows his nature. Since he is born spontaneously without anyone having asked him who or what he wished to be, nature wants him to return likewise to it, without having known either who or why." "Ah!" cried Yun Jiang, "heavenly being, you have enlightened me, transformed me. Throughout my life I have searched for the solution to the problem, and now I have it." That said, Yun Jiang prostrated himself with his forehead on the ground, got up, and went on his way. (Zhuang Zi, chapter 11.)

Nie Que asked Pi Yi to explain the Principle to him. Pi Yi said to him: 'Control your habits, concentrate your perception, and universal harmony will spread into you. Withdraw your faculties, unify your thoughts, and the vital spirit of the universe will live as a prolongation in you. The action of the Principle, communicating itself to you, will become the principle of your qualities. You will live in the Principle. You will acquire the simplicity of a new-born calf, and cease to preoccupy yourself with what you are and where you have come from. Before Pi Yi had finished his discourse, Nie Que had fallen into a profound sleep (carried away in ecstasy). Astonished, Pi Yi sang: 'See how his body has become like dead wood, and his heart like dead ashes. Having become transcendent, his true science no longer hesitates. Having become blind, his mind no longer debates. He has reached the intuition of the Principle. What a man!' (Zhuang Zi, chapter 22).

Yen Cheng Zi You said to Dong Guo Zi Qi: 'Since 1 have been your disciple, I have passed through the following stages: After a year I rediscovered my native simplicity. After three years I lost the sense of "you" and "I". After four years, I was indifferent and unfeeling. After five years, I began to live a superior life. After six years, my mind, entirely concentrated in my body, no longer wandered. After seven years, I entered in communion with universal nature. After eight years, I ceased to preoccupy myself with life and death. Finally, after nine years, the mystery was accomplished, I found myself united with the Principle.' (Zhuang Zi, chapter 27)

Reciprocity between the microcosm and microcosm.

(Music makes continuity between man and the whole of nature.) When Pao Ba touched his cither, birds danced and fish jumped. Shi Wen (who later became the chief musician of Zheng) wished to acquire the same talent, and left his family in order to become attached to Shi Xiang. First he spent three whole years exercising his fingering and touch, without playing a single note. Judging him to have little ability, Shi Xiang ended by telling him he could go back home. Putting down his cither, Shi Wen said with a sigh: "No, I am not without ability; but I have an aim, an ideal higher than ordinary classical playing; I am still unable to communicate to others the influence coming from my heart; that is why I dare not make my cither resonate; it wouldn't yet make the sounds I want. If I must leave, I shall do so; but it will only be for a time; we shall see each other soon." Not long after, Shi Wen came back to Shi Xiang. "How goes your playing?" asked the latter. "I have found my ideal," said Shi Wen; "you are going to see." It was then springtime. Shi Wen played the chord Shang, which responds to the pipe Nan and the season of autumn; straight away a cool wind blew and the fruits ripened. When, in autumn, he played the chord Jiao, which responds to the bell Jia and to the season of spring, a warm wind blew, and the plants flowered. When, in summer, he played the chord You which responds to the bell Huang and the season of winter, snow began to fall and the watercourses froze. When, in winter, he played the chord Zheng, which responds to the pipe Rui Pin and the season of summer, flashes of light shone and the ice

melted. Finally, when he played the four chords simultaneously, a gentle breeze blew, graceful clouds floated in the air, a sweet dew fell and winey springs gushed from the earth. Beating his chest and bowing (showing signs of regret), Shi Xiang said: "How well you play. It equals or surpasses in strength that of Shi Kuang and of Zi Yen. In your presence these masters should put down their cithers, and pick up the flageolet, in order to accompany you." (Lie Zi, chapter 5.)

5. NATURE AND CONVENTION

When action conforming to the Principle dwindles, (when men cease to act with spontaneous goodness and fairness), artificial principles of goodness and fairness, prudence and wisdom (are invented). These artificial principles soon degenerate into politics.

When parents no longer live in natural harmony, they try to make up for this deficit by inventing artificial principles of filial piety and paternal affection.

When states had fallen into disarray, they invented the loyal minister stereotype. (Lao Zi, chapter 18).

(The commentators say that conventional morality, with its principles and precepts, useless in the age of spontaneous goodness, was invented when the world fell into decadence, as a remedy for that decadence. The invention was somewhat unfortunate. The only true remedy would have been to return to the original Principle.)

Reject (artificial, conventional, political) wisdom and prudence, (in order to return to primordial natural uprightness), and the people will be a hundred times happier.

Reject (artificial, conventional) goodness and fairness, (filial and fraternal piety), and the people will come back (for their well-being, to natural goodness and fairness), to spontaneous filial and paternal piety.

Reject art and gain, and evildoers will disappear. (With the primordial simplicity, they will return to primordial honesty). Renounce these three artificial categories, for the artificial is good-for-nothing.

Be attached to simplicity and naturalness. Have few personal interests, and few desires. (Lao Zi, chapter 19)

That which is superior to the virtue of the Principle (the Principle itself, considered in its essence), does not act, but holds virtue in a state of immanence within itself. All those which are inferior to the virtue of the Principle (artificial rules of conduct), are only a palliative for the loss of that virtue; a palliative with which it has nothing in common.

That which is superior to the virtue (the Principle), does not act in detail. (The artificial rules) which are inferior to the virtue (of the Principle) only exist for action in detail.

When nature, with its natural good instincts, has been forgotten, artificial principles come as palliatives for this deficit. These are, in descending order, goodness, fairness, rites and laws.

Rites are but a poor expedient to cover up the loss of original uprightness and frankness. They are more a source of trouble (in etiquette and rubric) than they are of order.

The last term of this descending evolution, political wisdom (making laws), was the beginning of all abuses.

He who is truly a man, holds himself to uprightness and natural good sense. He is contemptuous of artificial principles. Using discernment, he rejects this (the false), in order to embrace that (the true). (Lao Zi, chapter 38)

Attempting to restore nature to its original state, by the studies that are undertaken in the present-day schools; wishing to regulate people's inclinations by enlightening them with classical reason shows a great blindness. The ancient sages knew of science only that it emanated spontaneously from the calm of their nature, a simple sensing of things, which did not trouble them. Their natural reason, derived from the Principle, functioned normally in their interior peace. Thus these quite simple notions were born: Goodness, supporting everything; fairness, being reasonable. From fairness came loyalty; the frank truth produced joy and its expression in music; mutual confidence produced politeness and its expression in the rites. Later on, rites and music became falsified, an element of perversion, which happens to everything that no longer conforms to nature. Right at the beginning men were simple and natural. There were no disorders from natural physical forces. The course of the seasons was regular so that no one suffered, and there were no premature deaths, theories, or sciences. That was the age of perfect unity and union, of men with each other, and with nature. No one interfered with the natural order and everything followed its course spontaneously. However decadence came. It began with the institutions of Sui Ren and Fu Xi (artificial production of fire, laws of family and marriage) which seemed to be a progress but which inaugurated the ruin of the primordial simplicity and promiscuity. Decadence increased at the time of Shen Nong and the Yellow Emperor (abandoning of nomadic life for agriculture, and formation of the state). Well-being increased, but at the expense of the ancient spontaneity. The decadence increased further when Yao and Shun reigned, introducing systematic correction (through laws and schools) and the obligatory practice of a conventional so-called goodness. The period of primitive ways was finished. Since then men have substituted theories in place of their inborn instinct, and peace has disappeared from the world. Now the progress of the arts and sciences has done away with what remained of natural simplicity, and people's minds have been filled with distractions. Now everything is disorder and perversion.

From this historical review, it follows that the adoption of conventional ways has been the ruin of primitive ways, and this ruin of primordial nature has been the ruin of the world. Nature and convention are two irreconcilable contradictions. The followers of these two ways cannot live in the same house together. They cannot even understand each other since they do not think or speak in the same way. A sage of the part of nature (a Daoist) would not need to hide himself in the mountains and woods; living amongst his fellow citizens, he would be unknown because he would not be understood. This state of things is not recent; it dates from quite a long time ago. The ancient sages that are commonly known as the hidden ones, did not make themselves invisible, nor keep their mouths closed, nor deliberately hide their wisdom. They did not hide themselves. It was their complete opposition to their times that hid them, making them pass unperceived, unknown, and misunderstood. In favourable times they could perhaps have reformed the world by returning it to its lost simplicity. But since unfavourable times prevented them from doing this, they spent their lives keeping the notion of primitive perfection to themselves, and waited in peace. These men did not look for knowledge varied by subtle differences, as do the present-day sophists; they did not wish to know all, or to do all. Somewhat reserved, almost timid, they kept themselves in their rightful place, meditating on their nature. The subject is, moreover, sufficiently vast to occupy a man, and sufficiently difficult to require discretion. To set oneself up as a master of the doctrine of the Principle with imperfect knowledge and conduct, would be to deny the doctrine, not to serve it. They worked therefore on their own self, taking all their happiness from their movement towards the goal. They did not dream, like the ambitious (Confucians) of our times, of grades and distinctions. What can these artificial things do for the perfection of nature? Nothing at all! They even give little satisfaction, for, being clearly precarious, those who have obtained them cannot be sure that they will keep them. The sages are equally indifferent to fortune or distress, neither rejoicing nor being saddened by anything. When a gain makes one rejoice, when a loss saddens one, it is a sign that one likes the object, affection and sadness being two disorders. Those who show their affection to any beings whatever; who do violence to their natural instinct for no matter what convention; such people do the opposite of what they should do. They should only follow their instinct, and live absolutely detached. (Zhuang Zi, chapter 16).

Whilst Zhuang Zi was visiting Duke Ai of Lu, the latter said to him: 'There are many scholars in the Duchy of Lu, but none, master, are comparable with you.' 'There are only a few scholars in the Duchy of Lu,' replied Zhuang Zi. 'How can you say that?' said the duke, 'when everywhere one sees men wearing academic costume.' 'The costume, yes,' said Zhuang Zi. 'They announce by their round bonnet that they know the things of heaven; by their square shoes that they know the things of earth; by their sonorous pendants that they know how to create harmony everywhere. Some know all of these things without wearing the costume. These wear the costume, without knowing the things. If you do not believe me, try an experiment; forbid, by edict, under pain of death, the wearing of this costume by anyone who has not the competence.' Duke Ai did this. Five days later, all but one of the scholars of Lu had changed their dress. The duke himself questioned this unique person on the government of the state. He replied to everything pertinently, without any possibility of being brought down. 'You were saying,' said Zhuang Zi to the duke, 'that there were many scholars in the Duchy of Lu; one is not very many.' (Zhuang Zi, chapter 21.)

Qing the sculptor made, for a peal of bells, a belfry whose harmonious beauty was a marvel to everyone. The Marquis of Lu went to admire it, and asked Qing how he did it. – 'Like this,' said Qing. 'When I received the commission to make the belfry, I concentrated all my vital forces, and withdrew myself completely into my heart. After three days of this exercise, I had forgotten the praise and remuneration that I would receive for this work. After five days, I no longer hoped for success, and I no longer feared failure. After seven days I had lost even the notion of my body and limbs, and entirely forgotten your highness and his courtesans; all my faculties were concentrated on their object and I felt that the moment for action had come. I went into the forest and contemplated the natural shapes of the trees, the most perfect from amongst them. When I had become fully permeated with this ideal, only then did I put my hands to work. That was what directed my work. It was through the fusion of my nature into one with that of the trees, that this belfry has the qualities which make it admired....'

Chui the craftsman drew free-hand circles as if they had been drawn with a compass. That was because he had come to draw them without thinking of them; in consequence his circles were perfect like the products of nature. His mind was concentrated on one, without preoccupation or distraction. A shoe is perfect when the foot does not feel it. A belt is perfect when the waist does not feel it. A heart is perfect when, having lost the artificial notion of good and evil, it does good naturally and abstains naturally from evil. A mind is perfect when it is without interior perception, without tendencies towards anything exterior. Perfection is to be perfect without knowing it (like unconscious nature). (Zhuang Zi, ch. 19.)

Prince Yuan of Song wanted a map and the scribes who had been summoned presented themselves, received their instructions, saluting; then, those who were discouraged went away; the others licked their brushes and stirred their ink, with a thousand airs and graces. One scribe who had come late with a nonchalant air, also received his instructions, saluted, and immediately retired to his cell. The duke sent to see what he was doing. They ascertained that he was at his ease, stripped to the waist, his legs crossed, and beginning by resting himself. When the duke heard this, he said: 'This one will succeed; he is a man who knows how to go about things.' (One succeeds by letting one's nature act.) (Zhuang Zi, chapter 21).

At the age of eighty-four the man who forged swords for the ministry of war had still not lost his dexterity. The minister said to him: 'You are skilled; tell me your secret.' 'It consists uniquely in always doing the same work,' replied the blacksmith. 'The taste for forging swords came to me when I was twenty. I only have eyes for that objective. I apply myself only to that. By dint of forging swords, I have ended by forging them without thinking of them. Whatever one does, when one does it without cease it ends up by becoming unreflected, natural, and spontaneous (and in consequence it conforms to the unreflected and spontaneous influence of the Principle); such action succeeds always.' (Zhuang Zi, chapter 22.)

He who holds in himself perfect virtue (without lust or anger) is like the new-born child whom the scorpion does not bite, the tiger does not devour, the vulture does not seize, and all respect. A child's bones are weak, its tendons are feeble, but it grasps objects strongly (just as its body and soul are held together by force). He has not yet any notion of the act of generation, and, in consequence, keeps his seminal virtue intact. He cries softly all day long without becoming hoarse, so perfect is his peace. Peace makes for durability; one who understands this is enlightened; whereas any violent excitement, above all lust and anger, wears one out. From this it follows that virility (which man abuses) is succeeded by decrepitude. Intense life is contrary to the Principle, and in consequence prematurely mortal. (Lao Zi, chapter 55. — The commentators say that the above chapter condemns lust and anger as being the greatest causes of decrepitude and premature death.)

6. THE SAGE

Ancient sages; true men.

The ancient sages were subtle, abstract and profound, in a way that cannot be expressed in words. Therefore I am going to use illustrative comparisons in order to make myself as clearly understood as possible.

They were circumspect like one who crosses an ice-covered river, prudent like one who knows that his neighbours have their eyes on him; reserved like a guest in front of his host. They were indifferent like melting ice (which is neither one thing nor the other). They were unsophisticated like a tree trunk (the rough bark of which conceals the excellent heartwood). They were empty like a valley (with reference to the mountains that form it). They were accommodating like muddy water, (they, the clear water, not repelling the mud, not refusing to live in contact with the common people, not forming a separate group).

(To seek purity and peace by separating from the world is to overdo things. They can be found in the world). Purity is to be found in the trouble (of this world) through (interior) calm, on condition that one does not let the impurity of the world affect oneself. Peace is to be found in the movement (of this world) by one who knows how to take part in this movement and who is not exasperated through desiring that it should be stopped.

One who keeps to this rule of not being consumed by sterile desires arising from one's own fancy will live willingly in obscurity and will not aspire to renew the world. (Lao Zi, chapter 15).

Ancient sage-rulers.

Faithful imitators of heaven and earth, of the Principle and its influence, the ancient rulers did not intervene directly or occupy themselves with details. It was because of this that they were able to govern the whole empire. Inactive, they let their subjects act. Immobile, they let men move themselves. Their thought extended to everything, without their thinking of anything; they saw everything in principle, without distinguishing details; their power, capable of anything, was applied to nothing. Just as the non-action of heaven and earth causes beings to be born and grow; so the ruler's non-action makes his subjects prosper. How transcendent is the influence of heaven, earth and such a ruler. And there is reason for saying, in this sense, that the ruler's influence unites itself with that of heaven and earth. Indefinable like that of heaven and earth, it attracts all beings and moves the mass of humans. Unique in its superior sphere, this influence spreads itself as it descends. The ruler formulates the abstract law; his ministers apply it to concrete cases. Military art, laws and sanctions, rites and customs, music and dances, weddings and funerals, and other things that torment the Confucians; all of these are minute details which the sage-ruler leaves to his officials. One must not think, however, that there are in human affairs neither degrees nor subordination, nor succession. There is a natural order based on the reciprocal relationship of heaven and earth and on cosmic evolution. The ruler is superior to the minister, father to son, older to younger brothers, old people to young people, man to woman, husband to wife; because heaven is superior to earth. In the cycle of the seasons, the two productive seasons precede the two unproductive ones; each being passes through two successive phases of vigour and decline; all this comes from the fact of cosmic evolution; and it follows that parents have precedence in the family, rank comes first at court, the old are honoured in the village, the wisest are entrusted in human affairs. To be lacking in these things would be to lack respect for Dao, the Principle, from which these rules have been derived. (Zhuang Zi, ch. 13).

Politicians; transcendent men.

The great concern of common politicians is to attach themselves to people; they wash their hands of those who will not make common cause with them. Since they prefer those who share their opinion, and detest those who are in opposition, it happens that they seek only, in fact, their own elevation. When they have achieved the object of their ambition, are they truly superior to the common people? Are they useful to the country? Imposing on the people what they are pleased to call their experience; is this not worse than abandoning them to themselves? Smitten with the idea of doing good to the principality which they administer after the system of the three ancient dynasties, they pay no attention to the vices of that system. Their enterprise exposes the principality to the gravest of hazards. It is lucky if it escapes. It has one chance of salvation in ten thousand. For one principality in which they succeed imperfectly, they absolutely ruin ten thousand others. Is it sad enough that the masters of the earth do not perceive this danger? The most important thing of all is within their grasp. They should not confide it to such limited and selfish people. If only they were to put their trust in transcendent men, in those who are free of all worldly interest, who come and go in space, walk in the nine regions, and who are citizens not of the country, but of the universe. They are the noblest men of all. The esteem of common men attaches to them just as infallibly as a shadow follows an opaque body, as an echo follows a sound. When he is consulted, the transcendent man exhausts the question by his reply, and makes good the wishes of the consultant. He is the resort of all the empire. His rest is calm and silent. His comings and goings are without determined aim. He leads on and brings back those he speaks with, without shock and through an impalpable influence. His movements have no fixed rules. Like the sun, he shines always. This man can be summed up by these words: He is one with the great whole. He is the great whole and is no longer himself. Having no particular existence, he no longer has any sense of ownership or possessiveness; the ancient emperors still had some. One must have none at all to become the friend of heaven and earth, to reach union. (Zhuang Zi, chapter 11).

Politics.

When he governs, the sage lets all people go free according to their several natures. He limits his action to the suppression of excesses which would harm the whole, such as power, wealth and ambition. (Lao Zi, chapter 29.)

(The suppression of excesses is the only intervention permitted to the Daoist, says the commentator Zhang Hongyang.).

One can govern with rectitude, one can wage war with competence, but it takes non-action to win and hold the empire. How do I know that this is so; from what I am going to say: The more rules there are, the less people enrich themselves. The more taxes there are, the less order there is. The more ingenious inventions there are, then the fewer serious and useful objects there are. The more detailed the penal code, the more thieves abound. Multiplication ruins everything.

Therefore the programme of the sage is quite the contrary. Not acting and the people amend themselves. Staying peaceful and the people rectify themselves; doing nothing and the people enrich themselves. Wishing for nothing, and the people come back to natural spontaneity. (Lao Zi, chapter 57).

Zhun Mang was going towards the eastern ocean, when he met Yuan Feng, who said to him: "What do you think of humanity? What are the politics of the lesser sages, the Confucians?" Zhun Mang answered: "They are to do good to all, favour the talented, rule the empire, and make the people obey, that is their politics." "And the politics of the Daoist sages, who collaborate with the cosmic influx?" asked Yuan Feng. "They are," said Zhun Mang, "not to make plans; to act under the inspiration of the moment; to count as nothing the artificial distinctions of right and wrong, good and evil; to give to everyone as one would give to orphans, waifs and strays in order to satisfy their needs, without expecting any return, without asking thanks of them, without even making oneself known." "And the politics of wholly superior transcendent men?" asked Yuan Feng. Zhun Mang said: "the latter fuse their spirit with the light, and their body with the universe. Their luminosity and emptiness is the total abnegation of the self. Submitted to their destiny, these men enjoy the disinterested joy of heaven and earth, practising non-intervention without love or hate, so that all goes spontaneously to its natural solution. Governed by them, all beings would return to their inborn instinct, and the world to its primordial state.' (Zhuang Zi, chapter 12.)

Jianglu Mian visited Master Ji Che and said to him: "The Prince of Lu asked me to advise him how to govern his principality well. I replied that you had not commissioned me for that. He insisted in order to have my personal advice. This is what I said to him; judge if I spoke well or badly. I said to the prince: 'Be dignified and sober; employ devoted officers and send away selfish egoists; if you do that, everyone will be on your side.'" Ji Che burst out laughing. "Your politics are as useful as the mantis that tried to stop a carriage," he said. "What you said is absolutely useless, and could be harmful." "But what then is the art of governing?" said Jianglu Mian. "This is how the great sages conducted themselves," said Ji Che. They encouraged the people to improve themselves, to advance themselves, by inspiring them with the taste for improvement and advancement; leaving them to evolve spontaneously and letting them believe that they wished and acted by themselves. That is great politics. These men did not rule at the time of old Yao and Shun (so extolled by Confucius), for they are more ancient than these venerable persons. They were of primordial origin, and their politics consisted in bringing back to life the spark of cosmic virtue residing in everyone's heart." (Zhuang Zi, 12).

Men Wu Gui and Chi Zhang Man Ji had watched Emperor Yu's army march past them. Man Ji said: "If this emperor were as good as old Shun, he wouldn't have to make war." "Did Shun reign during a troubled or a peaceful epoch?" asked Wu Gui. "You are right," said Man Ji; "there are no grounds for comparison. Shun reigned during an epoch so peaceful that anyone could have passed himself off as emperor. He wasted his time over trifles, such as curing ulcers, restoring hair, and caring for the sick. He drugged the empire with all the anxiety of a son who drugs his father." The Confucians praise him for his actions. A true sage would have been ashamed to act like that. At the time of perfect action, they made no special case of wisdom or ability. Governments were like the branches of great trees, which sheltered and protected without knowing or wishing to know it; the people were like wild animals that took refuge under these branches and benefited from their shade, without thanking them. The governments acted equitably without knowing the word equity, charitably without knowing the word goodness, loyally and faithfully, simply, and without asking for payment in return. In view of their extreme simplicity, no striking facts have come down from those times, and their history has never been written. (Zhuang Zi, ch. 12.)

The way of the sage.

One should become indifferent to veneration and outrage; and hold oneself always in natural equilibrium. One should be indifferent before making any effort, before acting; such that the effort, the action, arising from non-effort, non-action, is natural. In order to enjoy peace, one should keep one's body in good order. In order that the vital spirit should function properly, one should put one's heart completely at ease. In order always to act well, one should come out from one's rest only when one cannot do otherwise. This is the way of the sage. (Zhuang Zi, ch. 23.)

Know yourself.

Knowing others is wisdom, but knowing oneself is superior wisdom, (one's own true nature being most hidden and profound). Imposing one's will on others is strength, but imposing it on oneself is superior strength (one's own passions being the most difficult to subdue). Being satisfied (content with what destiny has given) is true wealth; being master of oneself (and bending oneself to the dispositions of destiny) is true character.

Staying in one's natural place (that which destiny has given) makes for a long life. After death, not ceasing to be is true longevity (which is the lot of those who have lived in conformity with nature and destiny). (Lao Zi, ch. 33).

(The commentary on the above chapter says that life and death are two forms of being, and that in the last part of this chapter it is a question of conscious survival after death).

Those who build on disinterestedness will not find their work destroyed. Those who keep themselves disinterested will not lose what they have. Their sons and grandsons will make offerings to them without interruption.

First of all one should conform oneself to the Principle; afterwards, this conformity will spread spontaneously, by itself, to one's family, district, principality, and the empire.

Through one's own nature one understands those of other individuals and of all individual collectives such as families, districts, principalities, and the empire.

How can one know the nature of an entire empire? By this! (through one's own nature). (Lao Zi, chapter 54).

The sage's formation.

When Lie Zi became a disciple he spent his first three years trying to rid himself of making judgments and qualifying in words. At the end of that time his master Lao Shang honoured him for the first time by looking at him. After five years he neither judged nor qualified even mentally; then Lao Shang smiled at him for the first time. After seven years, when he had forgotten the distinction of yes and no, of advantage and disadvantage, his master made him sit on his mat for the first time. At the end of nine years, when he had lost all notions of right and wrong, of good and evil, and of himself and others; when he had become absolutely indifferent to all, then he found perfect communion between the exterior world and his own interior. He ceased to make use of his senses (but knew all through superior, universal and abstract science). His spirit solidified as his body dissolved, his flesh and bones liquefied (etherized); he lost all sensation of the seat on which he was sitting, of the ground on which his feet were pressing; he lost all knowledge of fixed ideas, of spoken words; he reached that state where the mind is no longer moved by anything. (Lie Zi, chapter 4).

The sage, united with the Principle.

Guan Yin Zi said: "All things are clearly revealed to those who dwell in the nothingness (of interior form, in an indeterminate state). They are sensitive to their impression like a calm lake; they reflect them as in a mirror; they repeat them like an echo. United with Dao the Principle, they are in harmony with all things; they know all through general, superior reasoning, and in consequence they no longer use their senses to know individual things and details. The true reason for things is invisible, ungraspable, indefinable, and indeterminable. The spirit alone, returned to the state of perfect natural simplicity, can see partially into it when in deep contemplation. After this revelation, they no longer wish for, or to do, anything, which is true knowledge and true talent. Those who have seen the nothingness of all desire and all actions, what can they wish for, what can they wish to do? Even if they were to limit themselves to picking up a clod of earth or dealing with a handful of dust, they would still have been unfaithful to their principles, for they would have acted." (Lie Zi, ch. 4).

Water, the model.

Transcendent goodness is like water.

Water likes to do good to all beings; it does not struggle for any definite form or position, but puts itself in the lowest places that no one wants. By this, it is the reflection of the Principle.

From its example, those who imitate the Principle lower themselves, sink themselves. They are benevolent, sincere, regulated, efficacious, and they conform themselves to the times. They do not struggle for their own interest, but yield. Therefore they do not suffer any opposition. (Lao Zi, chapter 8).

In this world there is nothing more supple and weak than water; and yet no one, however strong and powerful, can resist its action (corrosion, wear, wave action); and no being can do without it (for drinking, growth, etc.).

Is it clear enough that weakness is worth more than strength, that suppleness can overcome rigidity? Everyone agrees with this; but no one acts according to it. (Lao Zi, chapter 78).

The sage differs from ordinary people.

The sage differs from the common in that he lives peacefully and avoids things which cause him trouble. Ordinary people do quite the opposite, seeking trouble and fleeing from peace. For one who knows the Principle, it is still necessary to keep silent about it, which is difficult, says Zhuang Zi. Knowing, and remaining silent, is perfection. Knowing, and speaking, is imperfection. The ancients tended towards the perfect. Zhu Pingman learnt the art of killing dragons from Zhi Liyi. He paid his entire fortune of one thousand pieces of gold for this formula. He practised for three whole years. When he was sure he had mastered it, he never did nor said anything. 'Then what's the good of it? When one is capable, one must show it,' say the common people. The sage never says 'must.' From 'must' comes trouble, wars, and ruin. Entangled in multiple details, encumbered by material worries, the mediocre person cannot tend towards the Principle of all things, towards the great incorporeal unity. It is reserved for the superior one to concentrate on what was before the beginning, to rejoice in contemplation of the obscure and indeterminate primordial being, such as it was then when there were only the formless waters, surging forth in unmixed purity. O humanity, you are studying straw, and are ignorant of the great repose (in the total science of the Principle). (Zhuang Zi, chapter 32).

Charity, simplicity, humility.

Everyone says the sages are noble, despite their common air, an air which they give themselves because they are noble (to hide their nobility and not to attract envy to themselves). Everyone knows, on the contrary, how much those who pose as nobles are of little worth.

The sages prize three things and hold on to them: charity, simplicity and humility. Being charitable, they will be brave (within just limits, without cruelty). Being simple, they will be liberal (within just limits, without waste). Being humble, they will govern without tyranny.

The people of today have forgotten charity, simplicity and humility. They prize war, ostentation and ambition. This is like wishing to fail. It is like wishing to perish.

For it is the charitable aggressor who wins the battle (not the savage aggressor; it is the charitable defender who is impregnable (and not the pitiless warrior). Those that heaven wishes well are thereby made charitable. (Lao Zi, ch. 67).

Avoiding violence and arrogance:

In this world there are only two ways, that of subordination or deference, and that of insubordination or arrogance. These tenets have been defined by the ancients as follows: The arrogant ones show sympathy only to those lesser than themselves. The deferential ones like their superiors also. Arrogance is dangerous for it makes enemies for oneself; deference is sure, for it only makes friends. Everything succeeds for the deferential person in both private and public life; whereas the arrogant person has only failures. Thus Yu Zi said that power should always be tempered by condescension; that it is condescension that makes power last; that this rule permits one to prognosticate reliably about the prosperity or ruin of individuals or states. Force is not solid, whereas nothing equals the solidity of softness. Lao Dan also has said: "The power of a state brings ruin on it, just as the greatness of a tree calls for the felling axe. Weakness gives life, strength makes death." (Lie Zi, chapter 2).

One speaks in vain of the Principle to arrogant and violent people. They lack what is necessary to understand it; their vices prevent them from being able to be taught and helped. To learn, one must believe that one does not know everything. That is the indispensable condition. Age is not an obstacle, intelligence is not always a means; submission of the mind is the essential. An artist from Song took three years to sculpt a natural mulberry leaf in jade, for his prince. Lie Zi heard of this and said: "if nature took so long, there would be very few leaves on the trees." It is the same for the propagation of doctrines; the sage goes back to the power inherent in the truth, not to artificial art. (Lie Zi, chapter 8).

Keeping away from degenerates and fakes:

A certain Cao Shang, a politician of Sung, was sent by his prince to the King of Qin. He set off with a fairly modest equipage and returned with a hundred cart-loads of presents from the King of Qin whom he had greatly pleased. He said to Zhuang Zi: "I could never be content to live as you do down a village side street, badly dressed and with worn shoes, thin and emaciated through poverty and starvation. I prefer courting princes. It has just gained me one hundred cart-loads of presents." Zhuang Zi replied: "I know the King of Qin's tariff. He gives one cart-load of presents to the surgeon who opens an abscess for him; he gives five cart-loads to the one who licks his piles. The viler the service rendered to him, the better he pays. What did you do for him to receive even more than the man who licks his piles? Get out of my sight." (Zhuang Zi, chapter 32).

Shi Cheng Qi went to find Lao Zi, and said to him: "Having heard that you are a sage, I have made a long journey to come and see you. I have walked for a hundred days getting callosities on the soles of my feet, and now I find you are not a sage. For you keep the leftovers from your meals indefinitely; you have ill-treated your sister because the rats have stolen the left-over vegetables" (which she could have eaten). Lao Zi looked on absentmindedly, letting him speak and making no reply. The next day, Shi Cheng Qi went back to Lao Zi's house and said to him: "Yesterday, I blamed you. Your silence has made me reflect. Please excuse me for yesterday." "I am no more impressed by your excuses than by your blames," said Lao Zi. "I have delivered myself from all desire to be called learned, transcendent, wise. You could treat me like a cow or a horse and I would not respond. Whether what they say is true or false, letting people speak spares one the trouble of replying. It is my principle always to let people speak as they will. My silence of yesterday was an application of it." Shi Cheng Qi walked round Lao Zi, so as not to tread on his shadow; then, presenting himself before him, asked him what he should do to amend himself. Lao Zi rebuffed him with these words: "Counterfeit being, of whom all the airs and graces denote untamed passions and lawless intentions, what right have you to impose yourself on me and make me believe you desire and are capable of (Daoist) culture. Go! I have no more confidence in you than in any single one of the frontier brigands." (Zhuang Zi, chapter 13.)

Abhorrence of war:

Those who act as advisors to a prince should keep themselves from wanting to make war against a country. (For such action, calling for revenge, is always paid for dearly). Wherever the troops stay the land produces only thorns, having been abandoned by the farmers. Wherever a great army has passed, years of unhappiness (from famine and lawlessness) follow.

Therefore the good general is content to do only what he has to, (the least possible, moral rather than material repression). He stops as soon as possible, guarding himself from exploiting his force to the limit. He does as much as is required (to re-establish peace) not for his personal advantage and fame, but from necessity and with reluctance, without any intention of increasing his power.

Any height of power is always followed by decadence. Making oneself powerful is therefore contrary to Dao, the Principle (the source of duration). He who is lacking on this point will not be long in coming to an end. (Lao Zi, chapter 30).

Weapons are disastrous instruments. A wise prince uses them only with reluctance and from necessity. He prefers always a modest peace to a glorious victory.

No one should think that victory is a good thing. He who thinks that shows that he has the heart of an assassin. Such a man would not be fit to rule the empire. (Lao Zi, chapter 31).

There is no worse curse than a war waged with little or no reason, (which is sought after deliberately, and pushed beyond necessary limits). He who does that, exposes his own goods to loss and causes great mourning. (Lao Zi, ch. 67)

Living by the imperceptible.

A wheel is made of thirty perceptible spokes, but it turns due to the imperceptible axis of the hub.

Vessels are made of perceptible clay, but it is their imperceptible hollow that is useful.

The imperceptible holes which make the doors and windows of a house are its essentials.

It is the imperceptible that produces effects and results. (Lao Zi, chapter 11).

(The commentaries on the above chapter state that man does not live by his perceptible body, but by the two imperceptible souls, the spermatic and the aerial. Therefore the Daoist takes care above all of these two invisible entities. The common people either disbelieve in them, or pay little attention to them because they are invisible. They are preoccupied with perceptible, material things. Now in many perceptible things, says the text, the useful, the effective, is what they have of the imperceptible, their hollow, a void, a hole. The commentators generalize in saying: Everything effective comes from a void; a being is only effective through its emptiness. It seems that the ancient wheels had thirty spokes because the month had thirty days).

Non-action:

Make of non-action your glory, ambition, business and science. Non-action does not wear one out. It is impersonal. It gives what it has received from heaven without keeping anything for itself. It is essentially a void. The superior man only exercises his intelligence like a mirror. He knows and understands without feeling attraction or repulsion, or it making a permanent impression on him. This being so, he is superior to all things and neutral with respect to them. (Zhuang Zi, chapter 7).

Under heaven is there or is there not a state of perfect contentment? Is there or is there not a means of lengthening the life of the body? What should one do or not do in order to attain this? The common people look for contentment in wealth, rank, longevity and the esteem of others; in repose, good living, good clothing, beauty, music and so on. They dread poverty, obscurity, shortening of life and ill-repute; lack of repose, good food, good clothing, beautiful sights and sounds. If they do not obtain these things they are saddened and afflicted. Is it not senseless to ascribe everything thus to the body? Some of these things are even exterior and foreign to the body, such as wealth accumulated beyond possible utilization, rank and the esteem of others. And yet for these things the common people use up their energy and torture themselves day and night. Truly worries are born with man and follow him all his life; even in the dullness of old age the fear of death does not leave him. Alone, the military officers do not fear death and they are held in esteem by the common people for it; rightly or wrongly I do not know, for if their bravery deprives them of life, it preserves the lives of their co-citizens; there is for and against. Civil officials who bring death on themselves by their impertinent criticisms are, on the contrary, blamed by the common people; rightly or wrongly I do not know, for if their outspokenness deprives them of life, it assures them of fame, there is for and against. As for the common people themselves, I avow that I do not understand how they draw contentment from that which contents them; the fact is that these things make them content but they do not make me content. For me, happiness consists in inaction whereas the common people rush about all the time. I hold as true the saying which goes: "Supreme contentment is to have nothing which contents; supreme glory is not to be glorified." Any act accomplished will be discussed and will be qualified as good by some and bad by others. Only that which has not been done cannot be criticized. In inaction there is supreme contentment which makes the life of the body last. Allow me to support my assertion by an illustrious example: Heaven owes its limpidity and earth its stability to non-action; conjointly, these two non-actions, heavenly and earthly, produce all beings. "Heaven and Earth," goes the saying, "do everything by doing nothing." Where is the man who has come to do nothing; that man will himself also be capable of doing everything. (Zhuang Zi, chapter 18).

Non-action does not mean nothing doing. Let everything do what it does, and then its nature will be satisfied. (Guo Mang).

The Carpenter is in non-action in carving wood, but he is in action in using the axe. The prince is in non-action in the management of affairs, but he is in action in the control of ministers. The ministers can manage affairs, while the prince can control ministers. The axe can carve the wood, while the carpenter can use the axe. Everything has its office. The high and the low both have their proper places. This is the perfection of the principle of non-action. (Guo Mang).

The sage does not wear himself out.

Keep your body and spermatic soul closely united, and ensure that they do not become separated.

Apply yourself such that the air you breathe in, converted into the aerial soul, animates the composite, and keeps it intact as in a new-born baby.

Keep yourself from considerations which are too profound, in order not to become worn out.

As for love of the people and anxiety for the state, limit yourself to non-action.

Let the gates of heaven open and close, without wishing to do something, without interfering.

Know all, be informed on everything, and for all that remain indifferent, as if you knew nothing.

Produce, rear, without taking credit for what has been produced, without exacting a return for your actions, without imposing yourself on those you govern. There you have the formula for transcendent action. (Lao Zi, chapter 10).

(The commentaries say that man has two souls, a double principle of life; first *pai* the soul coming from the paternal sperm, the principle of becoming and development of the embryo in the maternal womb. The more closely this soul clings to the body, the healthier and stronger is the new being. After birth, the absorption and condensation of air produces a second soul, the aerial soul, principle of subsequent development, and above all, of survival. In opposition to the rigidity of a corpse, flexibility here signifies life. The newly-born child is, for the Daoists, the ideal perfection of nature, still absolutely intact, and without any mixture. This infant is sometimes interpreted as an interior transcendent being, the principle of survival. Illness, excess, weakens the union of the spermatic soul with the body, thus bringing on the illness. Study, worry, wears out the aerial soul, thereby hastening death. Maintenance of the body and the aerial soul through cleanliness, rest and therapeutic breathing exercises are important items in the life of the Daoist).

If one keeps one's mouth and nostrils closed (to prevent evaporation of the vital spirit), one will reach the end of one's days without having suffered decadence. Whereas if one talks a lot and causes oneself much worry, one will use up and shorten one's life. (Lao Zi, ch. 52).

Walking in perfection.

When he was a young disciple, Lie Zi liked going for walks. His master Hu Zi asked him what he liked about walking. Lie Zi said: "In general it is a relaxation; many do it for the pleasure of looking around, I myself find pleasure in it by meditating; there are walkers and walkers; I myself differ from the common." "Not as much as you think," said Hu Zi; "for like the others you enjoy yourself. They enjoy themselves visually, you enjoy yourself mentally. There is a great difference between exterior meditation and interior contemplation. The meditative takes pleasure from nature, the contemplative takes it from within. The perfect walker takes from inside, the imperfect walker takes from things." After this lesson, Lie Zi thought it best to give up going for walks completely. "That is not what I meant" said Hu Zi; "go for your walks, but go perfectly. The perfect walker goes without knowing where he is going and looks without taking account of what he has seen. To go everywhere and look at everything with this mental attitude (of total abstraction, a complete view with nothing in detail); that is perfect walking and contemplation. I did not advise you to give up going for walks but to walk in perfection." (Lie Zi, chapter 4).

Independence.

Lie Zi was reduced to extreme poverty, and the signs of starvation could be plainly seen on his face. A visitor spoke of him to Zi Yang, prime minister of the Principality of Zheng, in these words: "Lie Yukou is a scholar versed in the knowledge of Dao. His poverty will cause it to be said that the Prince of Zheng does not look after his scholars." Piqued by this observation, Zi Yang immediately ordered the district official to send Lie Zi some grain. When the official's envoy presented himself at his house, Lie Zi greeted him most civilly but refused the gift. When he had left, Lie Zi's wife, striking her breasts with sadness, said: "A sage's wife and children should live in comfort and happiness. Until now we were hungry because the prince had forgotten us. Now it happens that he has remembered us and sent us food, which you have refused. Have you not acted against destiny?" "No!" said Lie Zi laughing. "I have not acted against destiny, for it was not the prince who sent us the grain. Someone spoke favourably of me to the minister, who sent it to us. If the same person had spoken unfavourably, he would have sent his hired killers just as stupidly. It was chance, not destiny; that is why I refused. I want to owe nothing to Zi Yang." Soon after this Zi Yang was killed by the people in an uprising.

Zeng Zi lived in the land of Wei. He wore an unlined robe of coarse cloth. His face betrayed suffering and hunger. The callosities on his hands and feet showed how hard he worked to live. He only had a hot meal once in three days. An article of clothing had to last him ten years. If he had tried to fasten his hat, the worn strap would have broken. If he had tried to put his entire feet into his shoes, the toe part would have come away from the rest. If he had pulled on the sleeves of his robe, they would have stayed in his hands. And none the less, dressed in rags and old shoes, he sang the hymns of the Shang dynasty in a voice which resounded in space like a bronze instrument. The emperor could not persuade him to serve as his minister, the great feudal lords could not persuade him to attach himself to them as a friend. His type was independent and free. He who would hold on to his freedom must renounce bodily comforts. He who would hold on to his life should renounce rank. He who holds to union with the Principle must give up all attachments.

Yuan Xian lived in the land of Lu, in a round makeshift hut with a wall of woven thorny bushes and a roof on which grass was growing. A mat fixed to a branch of a mulberry tree badly closed the opening which served as a door. Two jars with their bottoms out, set into the wall, closed by clear stretched cloth, formed the windows of its two cells. The roof leaked, the floor was damp. In this miserable den, Yuan Xian was seated contentedly playing the flute. Zi Gong went to pay him a visit, riding in a carriage so wide that it could not enter the lane, dressed in a white robe doubled with purple. Yuan Xian received him, a torn hat on his head, shoes with worn heels on his feet, leaning on a tree branch which served him as a walking-stick. On seeing him, Zi Gong cried out: 'How distressed you are!' 'Pardon!' said Yuan Xian. 'To lack goods is to be poor. To know, and not to do; that is to be distressed.' Zi Gong was reduced to silence. Yuan Xian added: 'Acting to please the world, making particular friends under pretext of the general good, studying in order to make oneself admired, teaching in order to enrich oneself, dressing oneself up in a disguise of goodness and fairness, going about sumptuously equipped; all the things you do are things I could never make myself do.'

Confucius said to Yen Hui: 'Hui, listen to me. Your family is poor; why don't you try to obtain a post?' 'No!' said Yen Hui, 'I don't want any position. I have fifty measures of land in the country, which provides my food, and ten measures in the suburbs, which provides my clothing. (Plants for textiles were cultivated near habitations to avoid theft during the night. The theft of cereals is more difficult). Meditating on your teaching, whilst playing the lute, suffices for my happiness. No, I will not try to obtain a post.' These words made a great impression on Confucius, who said: 'What a good mind Hui has! I knew well enough in theory that he who has modest tastes will not be encumbered; that he who only preoccupies himself with his interior progress is not affected by any privation; that he who tends towards perfection regards positions lightly. I have even taught these principles for a long time, but only now do I see them applied by Hui. Today, I, the theorist, have received a practical lesson.' (Zhuang 28).

When Zhuang Zi was fishing with a line on the banks of the River Pu, the King of Chu sent two of his grand officers to offer him the post of minister. Without pulling in his line, without taking his eyes off his float, Zhuang Zi said to them; "I have heard that in the temple of his ancestors the King of Chu carefully guards the carapace of a transcendent turtle sacrificed three thousand years ago to be used for divination. Tell me, if they had given it the choice, would this turtle have preferred to die so that its carapace would be honoured, or would it have preferred to live dragging its tail in the mud of the swamps." "It would have preferred to live dragging its tail in the mud of the swamps," said the two grand officers together. "Then go back to where you came from" said Zhuang Zi. "I also prefer to drag my tail in the mud of the swamps. I will continue to live obscurely, but free; I do not want a post which often costs the life of him who holds it and which always costs him peace." (Zhuang Zi, chapter 17).

Avoiding extremes.

Zhuang Zi said: "The natural dispositions of people are diverse. One cannot make a gregarious person live in solitude; one cannot make a solitary person converse. But absolute solitude or immoderate conversation are each unnatural; they are excesses. Misanthropes bury themselves alive; intriguers throw themselves into the fire. One should avoid these extremes. One should not, moreover, perform extraordinary acts, for once the circumstances under which they were performed are forgotten, history will perhaps judge them eccentric rather than heroic. Superior persons adapt themselves to the times and circumstances; they are not eccentrics, nor misanthropes, nor intriguers. They let people think and say without contradicting them, and keep their opinions to themselves." (Zhuang Zi, ch. 26).

Avoiding popularity:

When Lie Zi was going to Qi, he suddenly turned and retraced his steps. Bo Hun Wu Ren, whom he had met, said to him: "Why are you going back?" "Because I was afraid," said Lie Zi. "Afraid of what," said Bo Hun Wu Ren. "I had been in ten restaurants, and five times I was the first to be served. It must be that my interior perfection was visible to those people, for them to have served me before richer and older clients; I was therefore afraid that, should I go as far as Qi, the prince, having come also to know of my merit, would discharge on me the government that weighs so heavily on him." "Wisely thought!" said Bo Hun Wu Ren. "You have escaped a princely patron, but I fear you may yet find masters at home." Some time later, Bo Hun Wu Ren went to visit Lie Zi. He saw a quantity of shoes (an indication of the presence of so many visitors). Stopping in the courtyard he reflected at length, his chin resting on his stick; then he left without saying a word. However the porter had told Lie Zi. The latter quickly grabbed his sandals and ran after his friend without even taking the time to put them on. When he caught up with him at the outer gate he said: "Why are you leaving like this, without giving me any useful advice?" "What's the good of it now," said Bo Hun Wu Ren. "Did I not warn you? Now you have masters at home. No doubt you have not attracted them yourself but you have not kept them away either. What influence will you have on these people now? One can only influence by keeping at a distance. One can no longer speak frankly to those one is involved with. One cannot reprove those to whom one is tied. Common people's subjects of conversation are poison to the perfect man. What is the good of conversing with individuals that neither listen nor understand?" (Lie Zi, ch. 2).

The sage leaves all beings free.

They (the sages) let all beings become without thwarting them and let them live without monopolizing them and let them act without exploiting them.

They do not attribute to themselves the effects produced, and in consequence these effects last. (Lao Zi, chapter 2).

The Principle gives life; its virtue gives growth, protects, perfects, matures, maintains, and covers (all beings). When they are born it does not monopolize them; it lets them act freely without exploiting them; it lets them grow without tyrannizing them. This is the action of transcendent virtue (for imitation by the sage). (Lao Zi, chapter 51).

Incapacity protects.

The master carpenter Shi, travelling in the land of Qi, passed by the famous tree which shaded the mound of the earth genie at Qu Yuan. The trunk of this famous tree could hold a cow. It rose straight to a height of eighty feet, then spread out a dozen main branches, in each of which one could have dug out a canoe. People came in crowds to admire it. The carpenter passed close by without casting a glance at it. "But look!" said his apprentice. "Since I have wielded an axe, I have never seen such a beautiful piece of wood. And you ignore it?" "I saw it," said the master; "it is not suitable for making a boat, a coffin, a piece of furniture, a door or a column. Its wood is of no practical use. It will live a long time." When master carpenter Shi returned to Qi, he spent a night at Qu Yuan. The tree appeared to him in a dream and said: "Yes, trees that have good wood are cut down young. In the case of fruit trees, people break their branches in their ardour to ravish them of their fruit. Their usefulness is fatal to them. Therefore I am happy to be useless. It is the same for you men as it is for us. If you are useful, you will not reach old age." Next morning the apprentice said to the master: "If this great tree is content to be useless, why has it allowed itself to be made the genie of the place?" "They put it there," said the master, "without asking its opinion, and it laughs at that. It is not popular veneration that protects its existence, but its incapacity for ordinary use. Its tutelary action, moreover, amounts to doing nothing." (Such are the Daoist sages, put in place despite themselves, and keeping themselves from acting). (Zhuang Zi, chapter 4).

When Zhuang Zi was crossing the mountains, he saw a great tree with long and luxuriant branches. A woodman that was cutting wood nearby did not touch this tree. "Why not," asked Zhuang Zi. "Because its wood is good for nothing," said the woodman. "The fact of being good for nothing is valuable to this tree, allowing it to live until its natural death," concluded Zhuang Zi. After crossing the mountains, Zhuang Zi received hospitality at a friend's house. Happy to see him again, the master of the house told his domestic to kill a duck and cook it. "Which of our two ducks should I kill," asked the domestic; "the one that quacks or the mute one?" "The mute one," said the master. Next day, the disciple who accompanied Zhuang Zi said to him: "Yesterday the tree was saved because it was good for nothing; that duck was killed because it couldn't quack; therefore being capable or useless, which one saves?" "That depends on the case," said Zhuang Zi laughing. "One single thing saves in all cases; it is being elevated to the knowledge of the Principle and its action, and keeping oneself in indifference and abstraction. Such a man thinks as little of praise as of blame. He knows how to rise up like the dragon, and to flatten himself like a snake, bending himself to circumstances, not persistently taking any side. Should his position be elevated or humble, he adapts to his circumstances. He frolics in the bosom of the ancestor of things, Dao, the Principle." (Zhuang Zi, Ch. 20).

7. CONCLUDING EXTRACTS

(I have finished. Perhaps you may find my little discourse lacks something, is not very subtle, and is scarcely wise). This is because native frankness does not dress itself up, natural directness avoids quibbling, and common sense can dispense with artificial erudition.

The sage does not hoard, but gives. The more he does for people, the more he can do; the more he gives them, the more he has. Heaven does good to all, doing no evil to anyone. The sage imitates it, acting for the good of all, and opposing himself to no one. (Lao Zi, chapter 81).

Many recipes for governing the world have been invented by different authors, each one giving his own as the most perfect. It now turns out that all of them were insufficient. One procedure alone is effective, to allow Dao, the Principle to act without counteracting it. It is everywhere, penetrating everything. If the transcendent influences descending from heaven and rising from earth have produced sages, it is thanks to it, immanent in the universal whole. The closer a man is united with the Principle, the more perfect he is. The superior degrees of this union made celestial men, transcendent men, superior men. Then there came the sages, who knew speculatively that heaven was the way the Principle manifested itself to the senses; that the Principle was the origin of all, its action the root of all; and that everything came from it by way of evolution and return. Finally the princes applied these ideas in practice, through their beneficent goodness, their rational equity, the rites which rule behaviour, music which produces friendly understanding, a perfume of kindliness which penetrates all. Thus did the princes of antiquity, counselled by their sages. They distinguished cases and applied the laws to them. They qualified and denominated. They got to the bottom of all things through consideration and examination. Finally, all being clarified, they took measures as clearly defined as one can count one, two three. Because the hierarchy of officials functioned correctly, affairs followed their courses, and the care of the people became the great concern. Livestock rearing was encouraged, children and old people, orphans and widows, became the object of great anxiety; and all that could be done for the common good was done. In taking this trouble, the ancients collaborated with the transcendent influences of heaven and earth. They nourished the living, maintained peace, and extended their kindness to all. They drew their applications from perfectly fathomed principles, acting in all directions, on the most diverse things. The old laws which have been transmitted from age to age, and are conserved still in a great number of the histories, bear witness to the theoretical and practical knowledge of the ancients. Then there came the Odes, the Annals and the Rites, the treatises on music, the scholars of Tsou and Lu, and the official masters of principalities. According to them the Odes are a code of moral behaviour, the Annals a repository of facts, the Rites a rule of conduct, Music a means for producing concord, the Mutations (Changes) a means of knowing the movements of the yin and the yang, the Chronicles a means of distinguishing true reputation from false. Spreading from the central provinces throughout the entire empire, these writings have become the theme on which scholars exercise themselves. Then came the time when the empire had fallen into a great disorder, and being deprived of great sages, other principles were invented, debating commenced, and each one claimed to be right. It was like a dispute of the ears and eyes with the mouth and nose, which could never end in agreement, each sense being right, but only with regard to its own subject. Thus the different schools each have their own speciality, good in its time and place; but as none of them embrace everything, they have no right to exclude the others. How can a single scholar squatting in a corner, arrogate to himself the judgment of the universe and its laws, and everything that the ancients did and said? Who is qualified to set himself up thus as judge of things and affairs? Since the science of the Principle has fallen into neglect, people no longer act except under the influence of their passions, the chiefs of the various schools arrogating to themselves the right to judge and condemn all and everything. They lose sight of the primordial unity, which had been the great rule of the ancients. By their different explanations, they split up what was once the one teaching of the empire.

Let us speak now of the school of Guan Yin Zi and Lao Zi. Looking for pure causality in the invisible root of sentient beings, and considering these beings as gross products; considering their multitude as less than their Principle; dwelling withdrawn into one's spirit in emptiness and solitude; these are the maxims of the ancient science of the Principle. These maxims were propagated by Guan Yin and Lao Dan (Lao Zi). As a firm foundation for these maxims, they give the pre-existence of the infinite indeterminate being, the union of all in the great unity. From the principle of the being, from universal union, they deduced that the rules for human behaviour should be submission, acquiescence, non-wishing, non-acting, and non-intervening in order to do no harm. Guan Yin said: "All things appear in their truth to one who is not blinded by his own interests. The movements of this man are natural like those of water. The calmness of his heart makes it a mirror in which everything is concentrated. He responds to all events as the echo responds to the sound. He withdraws himself, effaces himself, accommodates himself to all and wishes nothing for himself. He does not push ahead of others, but keeps to being always the last." Lao Dan said: "Whilst fully conserving your male energy, submit yourself like the female. Make yourself the confluence of the waters. Being perfectly pure, accept seeming not to be so. Put yourself the lowest in the world. When everyone desires to be first, wish to be the last, and like the sweeper-up of the world. When everyone desires abundance, prefer indigence and seek after privation and isolation. Do not expend yourself; do not interfere. Laugh at those whom the common people call capable. Count yourself as nothing in merit, but be content to be irreproachable. Be ruled always by the Principle, and respect its laws. Avoid any show of strength or talent, for the strong are broken and the sharp are blunted by their enemies and those who envy them. Be big and friendly to all. This is the highest teaching." Oh Guan Yin! Oh Lao Dan! You were the greatest men of all times!

Let us speak now of Zhuang Zi. The old Daoists drew everything from the obscure and indistinct primitive being, from its alternating mutations, from the two states of life and death, from union with heaven and earth, from the departure of the spirit, from its comings and goings. Zhuang Zi takes up these subjects, and makes them his delights. He speaks of them in his own way, in original and bold terms, freely but without causing a schism. Considering that men find abstract lofty explanations difficult to understand he has recourse to allegories, to comparisons, to the putting on stage of characters, to repetitions of one and the same subject under diverse forms. Neglecting details of lesser importance, he attaches himself above all to the capital point of union of the spirit with the universe. In order not to draw useless discussions to himself, he neither approves nor disapproves of anyone. Sparkling with wit, his writings do not wound. Full of originality, his remarks are serious and worthy of attention. Everything he says is full of meaning. Two themes above all have his preference, they are the nature of the author of beings (Dao, the Principle) and the identity of life and death (successive phases). He has spoken about the origin with amplitude and elevation. On the genesis of beings and cosmic evolution his arguments are rich and solid. He sports himself in unfathomable depths. (Zhuang Zi, chapter 33).

REFERENCES.

Bryce, Derek and Weiger, Léon, the *Tao-Te-Ching of Lao Tzu with summaries of the writings attributed to Huai-Nan-Tzu, Kuan-Yin-Tzu and Kung-Hu-Ching,* Samuel Weiser, York Beach, 1999.

Cleary, Thomas, *Wen-tzu, Understanding the Mysteries, Further Teachings of Lao-tzu*, Shambhala, Boston & London, 1992.

Giles, Lionel, *Musings of a Chinese Mystic,* John Murray, London, 1906.

Graham, A. C., *The book of Lieh-tzu,* John Murray, London, 1961.

Goullert, Peter, *The Monastery of Jade Mountain,* John Murray, London, 1961.

Henricks, Robert G., *Lao-Tzu Te-Tao-Ching, a translation of the Ma-Wang-tui manuscripts pre-dating other texts by five centuries.* Rider, London, 1989.

Matgioi, *La Voi Metaphysique*, Les Editions Traditionelles, Paris, 1936.

Ni, Hua-Ching, *Heavenly Way*, Los Angeles, 1981.

Ni, Hua-Ching, *The Later Teachings of Lao-tzu*, Shambhala, Boston, 1995.

Ni, Hua-Ching, *Esoteric Tao The Ching,* The Shrine of the Eternal Breath of Tao, Malibu, California, 1992.

Ni, Maoshing, *The Yellow Emperors Classic of Medicine*, Shambhala, Boston, Mass. & London. 1995.

Watson, Burton, *The Complete Works of Chuang-tzu*, Columbia U.P., N.Y. 1968.

Wieger, Léon, *Les Pères du Système Taoiste*, Hsien-hsien, 1913; reprint Les Belles Lettres, Paris, 1950.

Wieger, Léon, *Histoire des Croyances Religieuses et des Opinions Philosophiques en Chine*, Hsien-hsien, 1917.

Wieger, Léon, *A History of the Religious Beliefs and Philosophical opinions in China,* trans. Edward Chalmers Werner, Hsien-hsien, 1927.

Wieger, Léon, *Wisdom of the Daoist Masters*, translated by Derek Bryce, Llanerch, Felinfach, 1984.

Yu-lan Fung, *Chuang Tzu,* Shanghai, 1931.